Energy Transition

Energy Transition

Second Edition

Bertrand Cassoret

CRC Press
Taylor & Francis Group
Boca Raton London New York

CRC Press is an imprint of the
Taylor & Francis Group, an **informa** business

Second edition published 2021
by CRC Press
6000 Broken Sound Parkway NW, Suite 300, Boca Raton, FL 33487-2742

and by CRC Press
2 Park Square, Milton Park, Abingdon, Oxon, OX14 4RN

© 2021 Bertrand Cassoret

First edition published by De Boeck Supérieur 2018

CRC Press is an imprint of Taylor & Francis Group, LLC

The right of Bertrand Cassoret to be identified as author of this work has been asserted by him in accordance with sections 77 and 78 of the Copyright, Designs and Patents Act 1988.

ISBN: 978-0-367-54278-8 (hbk)
ISBN: 978-0-367-54277-1 (pbk)
ISBN: 978-1-003-08848-6 (ebk)

Typeset in Times
by Deanta Global Publishing Services, Chennai, India

Contents

Foreword by Brice Lalonde

Brice Lalonde is president of the association *Equilibre des Energies*, France's former Environment Minister, former ambassador for international climate issue negotiations and former executive coordinator of the United Nations' conference on sustainable development.

It is an honour for any environmentalist to be invited to produce the preface of a book in which the author confronts some beliefs and visions commonly attributed to environmentalists with the laws of physics. It is stimulating while perilous. Encouraged by his obvious good faith, I have followed Bertrand Cassoret – a modern *Candide*[*] – in his overview of energy consumptions and sources as well as in his exploration of the possible options for their future, which is what energy transition refers to. A transition! Do we even know where it is supposed to lead us? It is one of those concepts so full of meaning that they end up dulling the sense. Is it like hobbling along a path bordering on collapse but leading to some ideal world? Or, more prosaically, weaning mankind off fossil fuels to preserve its best ally for a hundred centuries, the climate? This is the way I favour, scared as I am of a climate catastrophe, and outraged by the blindness of both the sceptic and the cynic.

Fossil fuels, coal, oil, natural gas, are primarily responsible for the ongoing global warming and its parade of disasters, but also for the tremendous prosperity of the past 300 years. No doubt they have contributed to the rarity of wars, famines and epidemics for the last half-century. A treasure to preserve! Thank them and ask them to go now. They still account for 80% of the global energy consumption. But, so far, humanity has never been confronted with such an accumulation of crises sprung from the destruction of nature. As a true pragmatist, Bertrand Cassoret is not unaware of the relevance of questioning an infinite growth within a finite world, but he focuses on energy, seen as one of the principles, if not the major principle of human progress. Energy is his job, he is familiar with it, he can see it everywhere at work. It is omnipresent in social activities, whether at home or in the economy, in all machines, in transport and communication systems, to such an extent that its presence is often little known or at least seen as normal and taken for granted, until it is brought back to our consciousness owing to a power failure, a strike or a price rise.

Phasing out fossil fuels to avoid climate-damaging emissions is managing the transition. Let us remember that the CO_2 – carbon dioxide – emitted whenever coal, oil or natural gas is burnt is the longest-lasting greenhouse gas in the atmosphere. The unburnt natural gas, or methane, has a more powerful and harmful action but, fortunately, a shorter lifespan. Sending CO_2 or natural gas into the air should thus be avoided. This simple objective should be the trail through the maze of everyday emergencies. Unfortunately it is in competition with, if not supplanted and eventually thwarted by, the endless pursuit of other aims instead of being supported by

---

[*] TN: From a philosophical tale by Voltaire: *Candide ou l'Optimisme* in which "Candide" is the name of a definitely ingenuous character.

them: reducing energy consumption and the use of nuclear power while increasing the share of renewable energies. Let us consider the situation in detail.

Though unanimity may well be expressed in favour of a reduction of energy consumption, it still seems to be stagnating. At least, if the GDP increases, it means that the amount of energy per point of growth decreases. Improvements in energy efficiency are always welcome, providing they do not provoke a rebounding effect: an economical car will allow you to use it more, which will wipe out any gain. But, reading the laws and some scenarios suggested towards a transition, the energy consumed by the French would have to be massively reduced, at least by half, in order to perhaps be able to content themselves with renewable sources. The feasibility of these scenarios is carefully scrutinized by the author who first questions the extent of a reduction that borders on scarcity.

Energy does not mean happiness, he writes, but it helps. Sobriety is a virtue. On the other hand, deprivation could trigger a major political crisis. The anger demonstrated by the "gilets jaunes" is to give food for thought. It is the demand, and not only the supply aspect that should be looked at. Let us review common uses of energy in everyday life. What will our homes be like, how shall we eat, dress, work, enjoy ourselves, communicate, come and go, take holidays? If our consumption is not tenable, what should we give up, how to cut consumption equitably? But, on the other hand, if energy can be decarbonized and produced cleanly, why should the French be prevented from taking advantage of it?

Deindustrialization and new markets have sent factories to Asia, thus increasing the French carbon footprint left behind by their imports. In this respect, reindustrializing this country could paradoxically contribute to reducing global emissions if Europe's environmental requirements are considered more demanding than elsewhere. Apart from industries, the major two greenhouse gas emission sources over the national territory are transport systems and buildings. This is therefore what our efforts must be focused on.

Today, the automobile industry is required to produce electrical vehicles, local authorities are required to install electric charging stations and everyone is to check for the clean production and recycling of batteries, while a complementarity will possibly be put in place between the vehicle, the house and the power network. The car battery will be charged during off-peak times and the power of the battery will be sold to the network in peak times. Simple! But where are the charging stations that will have to be compatible and connected? Where are the European battery-making factories? In fact not that simple! Let us add straightaway that during the years to come, the energy used by passenger cars will be electricity and not hydrogen because the latter would need to be produced cleanly. On the other hand, hydrogen has a bright future ahead as the companion for electrical power.

The future of energy shall mainly be electrical for three reasons: because electricity can – and must – be produced without CO_2, thanks to hydraulic, nuclear or renewable powers; because it replaces oil cleanly and efficiently in many uses (vehicles for example); and because it naturally lends itself to digitalization as its vector. And digitalization is the indispensable backup for a more complex electrical infrastructure. Today, electricity covers 25% of our final consumption. This figure should reach at least 50%. And the reason why hydrogen has a bright future is that it can offer the best electricity storage solution, thanks to water electrolysis: one way to have oil replaced by water! Ultimately, carbon-free hydrogen could become the universal fuel. It would first rise from electricity overproduction generated by the odds and ends of the network, then from dedicated power stations. It would travel as it is, or be carried by a larger molecule, in converted fossil fuel infrastructures.

As for buildings, the stock of which is renewed by 1% each year, their emissions are higher than the volume assigned by the public authorities according to the national low-carbon strategy. And it is simply because 80% of the new collective housing buildings are heated by gas. Surprising, isn't it? It is due to a nonsensical regulation called primary energy. The French regulation concerning buildings, referred to as RT 2012, states that all newly built buildings are assigned a maximum consumption of energy – measured as so-called primary energy – of 50 kWh per square metre per year. But electricity is therefore penalized, and electricity only, with a handicap requiring it to stay under 20 kWh, which consequently bans electrical heating installations.

What is the reason for this inequality? Because electricity does not exist in nature in an accessible form. It is not a primary energy. It has to be produced and energy has to be spent to produce it. This is perfectly true, but it is of no relevance in the French energy transition process if the priority consists in reducing climate-affecting emissions. On the contrary, this regulation hinders the objective as it blocks the way to carbon-free electricity while favouring fossil gas which is a CO_2 emitter.

The penalty might have been understandable when electricity was produced from fossil fuels, which is still the case in Germany, Poland and many other countries. As a matter of fact, it is more efficient to burn coal directly in one's boiler rather than in a power station producing the power we would then use for heating. Thus, saving fossil primary energy is meaningful. But everything is different with hydraulic, nuclear and renewable energy sources. Uranium is not attractive other than in a nuclear reactor, the same for a water reservoir behind a dam. So long as the major objective is to abandon fossil fuels, it is paradoxical to see that the French energy conservation policy regarding buildings leads to an increase in the consumption of gas and in CO_2 emissions.

In order to implicate French people into energy conservation efforts, it is logical to express the amounts consumed by buildings in final energy, i.e. the energy actually delivered and measured on the site where it is used. This is the very energy they know about and pay for, which they would therefore be able to save. Conversely, subject to an incomprehensible primary energy measure, they are prisoners of energy choices imposed upstream of the buildings by any central committee. Today, electric heating is all the more efficient as buildings have better insulation, as connected and controlled radiators replace old convectors and as the heat pump wins recognition as a nearly renewable energy source, providing three times more heating energy than the electricity it consumes. Why single out buildings for special regulatory measures while electrical power is encouraged for passenger vehicles? Probably because gas producers represent a powerful lobby group and energy efficiency doctrinaires hunt for calories, ignoring CO_2 emissions.

The path leading to the transition is not the bed of roses one might like to imagine. Bertrand Cassoret usefully approaches the matter in terms of nature's implacable laws. He is surprised that so-called experts do not take them into account. But human weaknesses and politics are involved. I have never come across a minister or a member of parliament who could understand the challenges of measuring primary or final energy within the time I was given to expound them. On the other hand, I have met many administrations and organizations who fight against nuclear energy rather than climate change, including ministers who revel in shutting down nuclear power stations on their own authority while they are still perfectly functional. The question is to know whether the share of nuclear energy is simply reduced for diversification reasons or definitely doomed to disappear by a process of elimination. What then would be the consequence of each branch of the alternatives of reducing emissions? Answers are crucial. Politicians must mark out the transition process. Industries need to organize themselves.

Nuclear energy: the elephant* in the transition process. There are definitely a few of us, environmentalists, who have decided to abandon or keep quiet about the hostility we used to show towards it. Climate change is so monstrous that we look at nuclear energy in a different light. Nuclear produces a lot of energy with very little CO_2. It takes up little surface area. Its impact is far lower than that of coal, which is a deadly energy source, or gas, which leaks to the detriment of the climate and blows up houses from time to time. Nuclear energy is thus very useful against climate change. It is high time antinuclear forces stopped racking their brains to deny the obvious. The systematic denigration of nuclear power is no longer in season.

The primary mission of environmentalists is to defend living conditions on the planet's surface, which are seriously deteriorating, hit in the first place by the climate imbalance which is the mother of all crises. To sum up: nuclear energy is a powerful ally against climate change. Fighting an ally instead of fighting the enemy means running the risk, like it or not, of becoming the latter's accomplice. I would not like environmentalists to dismiss nuclear energy out of dogmatism, to even favour fossil gas and to become the fifth column of climate change, making the fight more difficult to win. It would be tragic.

For all that, if nuclear energy is indispensable to the transition process, and perhaps beyond, it is not perfect. It is expensive. It handles dangerous products. It leaves long-lasting waste behind. Can it be improved? For my part, I think an international governance should be strengthened and waste transmutation be explored. If France adjourns the so-called Astrid fast-neutron reactor, it should cooperate in Myrrha, the project of an industrial prototype transmutation reactor located in Mol in Belgium. The aim of the transmutation process is to reduce the toxicity of waste by a factor of a thousand, down to the radiotoxicity of uranium as it is in nature after three centuries.

Of course, nuclear power is not the only carbon-free energy source. It currently outdistances hydroelectric power and other renewable energy sources, mainly wind and solar power. It will soon be outflanked by renewable energies or will

---

* T.N.: a metaphor referring to the Indian parable "The Blind Men and the Elephant".

more modestly supplement them, depending on the role they will play, whether primary or secondary. Bertrand Cassoret is harsh with them, noting that their power is inadequate, that their production of electricity is altogether rather low, obviously far lower than their theoretical capacity, despite the support they are granted. But the time of generous subsidies is coming to an end, and even if they are still frowned upon because of the materials they require ordered from China or Africa, there is no reason why we should deprive ourselves of what we can get from the wind and the sun when available. The advantage of renewable energy is to let us use the income granted by nature rather than exhausting the capital of fossil and mineral resources.

Just like doubting Thomas, all we have to do is observe the growth of installed power capacities around the world and in Europe to understand that this growth is evidence of their success. Renewable electrical energies are beginning to rearrange the landscape of electrical power. They are transforming the balance of networks, switching from a centralized architecture of huge power stations to a heterogeneous mishmash of installations of all sizes which is supposed to adapt to the whims of the sunlight and the wind. Renewable energy installations require heavy investment, but their day-to-day running is practically free. They benefit from a marginal cost pricing system (the cost of one more kWh) to impose themselves and bring wholesale electricity prices down to a level so low that investing in controllable installations is no longer possible. The European market rules should probably be reviewed. Renewable energy devices actually require a replacement solution in case of interruption, an installation that can be said to be controllable and activated on demand in case of deficiency. Or else a supplementary solution that is not yet available: the storage of electricity at the required scale and duration.

Today, photovoltaic energy becomes the cheapest source of electrical power. In the developing world, it is the key to accessible energy, and all the more so when there is no existing network. However, it is not yet able to supply large cities. Should we share the author's reservations? From the solar oven to the photovoltaic cell, solar energy can adapt to many configurations that have not yet been implemented. I am filled with admiration for the metamorphosis of the photon into an electron, without any combustion, without any pollution. But I sometimes wonder whether the mission of renewable energies in France does not mainly aim at ensuring local resilience with collective self-subsistence and mini networks, rather than supplying the large European grid with huge solar power stations and gigantic wind farms. Will the tall pylons and high-voltage power lines always withstand 190 mile/h winds? I am upset by the quest for gigantism as much as by the contempt wind-turbine promoters show for resistance movements. They are treated like nuclear power station protesters used to be in the old days. "Shut up! It's for your own good". Is it decent, in the name of ecology, to ban any objection to renewable energy installations as if they did not have any impact on the local environment?

Renewable energies cover many sources of energy. Most often, we speak of electric renewable energies, those which compete with the already carbon-free electricity produced by nuclear power. But renewable heat energy sources are sometimes overlooked, which reduces the market share of fuel-oil and gas, thereby helping the fight against climate change. These are thermal solar energy (the solar water heater) backed by well-exposed buildings – geothermal energy in all its forms, wood and biomass (with caution), the incineration of garbage linked to networks of urban heat, the recovery of the fortuitous heat gain from a number of industrial processes, even chimneys and wastewater, green gas and, as I said, the heat pump which is enjoying increasing success. If there is a priority to give to renewable energies, it is these.

The progression of electrical renewable sources is supported by their decreasing cost as well as by the widespread idea that the more renewable energy systems, the better our health. But here lies the snag again. Should we install an appropriate proportion of electrical renewable devices or should we head for an all-renewable future, as a response to yesterday's all-nuclear? Whenever a public organization releases a study stating that it will be possible to produce 100% of our energy through renewable means within a few decades, the press is happy, the transition ministers shout hosanna and the good news spreads. But finding out its biases requires a careful study. Bertrand Cassoret has worked hard to read them on our behalf. For sure, if the French reduced their energy consumption drastically, if days were long throughout the year, the sky without any cloud and trade winds blew continuously over the country, it would then probably be possible. It is to the author's credit to stand against the flow, to demonstrate that, short of a hardly imaginable reduction of consumption, renewable energies shall not be fit for purpose on their own.

In the present state of our techniques, the number and the surface area of renewable installations have to be evaluated to obtain a guaranteed electrical power – more than 1,000 wind-turbines are required to supply the guaranteed equivalent power of a nuclear power station – and to plan how to take over from them when there is no wind or sunlight. In Germany they use coal to make up for them, and this is the reason why the rise of renewable energies has so far just slightly helped reduce its CO_2 emissions. In France, the compensation relies on nuclear energy. But gas is becoming more and more talked about as the renewables' best friend thanks to its unequalled flexibility. We would then be in a mess if both the two linchpins of the French energy transition – primary energy saving and electrical renewables – led to the promotion of fossil gas. Such is the risk of getting the objectives mixed up. The fight against climate change has to come first. The priority is not to multiply renewables at all costs.

A chapter about carbon neutrality should also be written. Since the 2015 Paris Agreement, cutting emissions has been seen as insufficient. We still need to reach the carbon-neutrality stage, which means a balance between greenhouse gas emissions and their neutralization, particularly through the capture of the CO_2 emitted into the atmosphere, either by means of an artificial process or through photosynthesis. In the latter case, the plant biomass has to be increased, for example by planting trees which will construct their tissues with the CO_2 from the air. Forestry management and agriculture in general, the industrial version of which is far too oil-dependent, thus become energy transition actors. Burning too much wood must not decrease the forest surface area as the carbon well would be less efficient. This is but one more factor to add to the complexity of the policies to be put in place but also an opportunity for forestry staff and farmers. Perhaps industries will develop a CO_2 capture and recycling process which would be the basis of a new chemistry.

I do urge the general public – and the ministers – to read Bertrand Cassoret's book. He is worried about the findings he has come to while scrutinizing the energy current events and the energy transition options in France. He wishes to inform his fellow citizens about them. He would like to clear up the illusions of a fresh and happy transition. Al Gore had made the reality of climate change popular, under the headline: "An unconvenient truth". Bertrand Cassoret borrows the same words to make us aware that the energy transition, together with a few dreams that go with it, will inevitably meet with laws of physics, which will constrain our freedom of action.

The warning is a salutary one. Our authorities often content themselves with words. France is unable to follow the four-factor trajectory, i.e. a reduction of emissions by four. No big deal! The parliament has adopted the six-factor one. It will work better, for sure! The gap between words and reality is getting indecent. Isn't there going to be a time when the population will demand explanations? Greta Thunberg and her peers will soon be old enough to stand in general elections and take legal action.

With this preface, I wish to support the warning and alert to the risks created by the confusion in the French policy's objectives. Saving energy, reducing the share of nuclear and developing renewable energies are all programmes serving the fight against climate change. They are not goals as such, which should be carried out all the way through because, when pushed too far, they undermine the efforts made towards a reduction of CO_2. The dose makes the poison. A means should never be taken for an end.

Should we sink into pessimism? In my mind, the technical path forward is clear: decarbonized heat, carbon-free electricity and carbon-free hydrogen are together the goal to be reached by the end of the transition process, whatever the means used. We are not home and dry yet! There are a great many material and financial obstacles. Changes are difficult. There are some entrenched habits. But where things are the most difficult is in the political field. Fossil fuel industries pressure groups resist. The financial world is conformist. Errors are a waste of time, demagogy perverts the public opinion. This is not the aim of this work, which alerts us to the reality of energy but not to its politics. I am just mentioning them to fuel the author's next book.

Let me add that withdrawing into ourselves would undermine the transition. Climate change is a planet-wide issue. People will have to have two irons in the fire: to rely on their strengths and to cooperate. Unfortunately, the climate is getting unpredictable and violent. We will have to spend a growing share of our strengths to adapt. Since the establishment of the United Nations Framework Convention on Climate Change, meetings come one after another with an appalling inefficiency, but the non-state actors have taken over from negotiators. Businesses, local authorities, associations, French people, as others around the world, are inquiring and mobilizing and this book adds its contribution. There lies hope.

Brice Lalonde

Presentation by Professor Jacques Foos

Energy is indispensable to life and economic development, and the major challenge of this century will be to cover humankind's energy requirements. Is it possible?

Explaining this challenge in simple words that everybody can understand is hard work, but it is useful to help everyone understand clearly the issues at stake in the future.

This is the task Bertrand Cassoret has buckled down to successfully. He managed to find the simple words that illustrate the various aspects of energy and their links with all the other phenomena of our living conditions, whether they may be deliberate or not: first of all, the galloping demography we have met with for a century and which is not about to decrease.

At the end of the year 2011, we passed 7 billion inhabitants on the planet and there were 700 million more of us at the beginning of this year 2020, that is to say a daily rate of +230,000 with 400,000 births for 170,000 deaths! At this pace, there will be 10 billion earthlings in 2050, within less than 35 years. Some economists even base their analyses on 11 if not 12 billion individuals.

The demographic growth involves considering these populations' needs in water, food and education and of course health. Yet, everything brings you back to energy. Feeding the planet's inhabitants relies on the amounts of water, fertilizers and soils available. There again, the thirst for energy is huge. We know how much the choices in the assignment of lands – between what will be devoted to the production of food or of biofuels – are crucial. The starvation riots that occurred in some developing countries are mainly due to the speculation on cereals initiated by "richer" countries anticipating a growing demand for them.

What about education? In many villages in India, the community leader starts up the only power generator for one hour in the evening. How can the young pupils do their homework? In those countries, and in those countries alone, the future lies in the development of photovoltaic power.

Health is also a matter of energy: birth rates may be one demonstrative example. A woman giving birth to a child on her own in an African village without any medical assistance will have consumed some 90kWh throughout the nine months of her pregnancy. A woman giving birth to her child in a "richer" country after regular medical visits, ultrasound scanning and a delivery in a maternity ward consumes an energy equivalent to about 4,000 kWh – 45 times as much – but put to good use. Our hope in the future is to see all women benefit from that medical assistance.

The evolution of the world population will lead to a huge increase in the consumption of energy. We must not only follow the demographic curve but go beyond for a better response to the populations' needs in developing countries.

Let us keep in mind that the current world we belong to is unfortunately easy to describe when referring to its inequalities: one-fifth of the population – including us – spends four-fifths of the total energy currently produced by this planet. Yet, at least two other fifths are accounted for by really poor developing countries including 2.8 billion earthlings. These people's energy requirements are so huge that we must take them into account.

Just by accounting for the increase observed for the 20th century – 2.35% per year – we get to an annual requirement up to three times as high as our consumption throughout the years 2000 to 2010. How could we consider that the rate of the world's consumption of energy is likely to be lower than in the 20th century which started with a population of 1.6 billion. With a lot of humour and real efficiency, Bertrand Cassoret criticizes the lack of credibility of the scenarios that would take us back to the Middle Ages!

This means that humankind can't do without any energy source, whatever it may be.

Since the Paris Agreement and COP 21, humankind has been aware of global warming, a prelude to various climate deregulations. Since then, similar international meetings have taken place every year, gathering thousands of delegates and observers representing 200 countries or so joined by over a hundred NGOs to a scale never seen before and a scale commensurate with the challenge for the future of our planet. But, because economic considerations intertwine with the probably vain wishes, while decisions take a long time to make, state and government leaders' speeches have led to a consensus: the big winner of that conference is decarbonated energy.

Indeed, managing to take up the challenge of limiting the overall increase of the planet's temperature, greenhouse gas emissions have to be drastically reduced, mainly CO_2 but also other gases such as methane which is even more harmful in that field. Hence the word "decarbonated", which used to be unknown in any dictionary but has become very common nowadays. It is difficult in many cases, such as for domestic heating or air and sea transport systems, to do without fossil energy, but it is 100% possible for the production of electricity.

Let us put ourselves in the shoes of a political leader who happens to be interested in the production of decarbonated electricity. Amongst the various energy sources, he will favour the most reliable one, the more economical one – with a high electrical power output – the safer one – with the highest possible control – with the lowest ground surface area requirement, the most respectful to the environment on the whole.

He will choose – and it is already well on its way! – the electronuclear production process and all the more so as intermittent energy sources – photovoltaic and wind-turbines – are all consumers of our planet's rare metal resources. "Sustainable development", did I hear you say?

Many countries turn to nuclear energy everywhere around the planet. There have never been as many reactors being built as there are today, not mentioning projects in the pipeline!

Here again, Bertrand Cassoret goes through the full range of energies with an implacable logic, without any passion, with no militancy on either side, just with a fully scientific rigor and great common sense.

He is offering the reader, who will surely devour his book, the opportunity to make up their own clear and simple opinion about energy problems and feel strengthened with a better understanding of the various debates on subjects they will obviously be confronted with.

Jacques Foos,* January 2020
Honorary Professor, Conservatoire National des Arts et Métiers
Director of Société Nationale des Sciences Naturelles et Mathématiques
(Cherbourg)

---

* Latest works published: "Peut-on sortir du nucléaire?" written in collaboration with Yves de Saint Jacob (éditions Hermann, Paris, October 2011, 270 pp.), *Prix du Forum Atomique Français* 2012 and "Regard sur la Société d'aujourd'hui" (éditions Hdiffusion, Paris, April 2019, 260 pp.)

Acknowledgements

I wish to thank:

Brice Lalonde, president of the association *Équilibre des Energies*, France's former Environment Minister, former ambassador for international climate issue negotiations and former executive coordinator of the United Nations' conference on sustainable development.

Jacques Foos, honorary professor at *Conservatoire des Arts et Métiers*, physician, former director of CNAM's Nuclear Research Laboratory, for his support, the review of this book and the writing of its preface.

My colleague Professor Raphaël Romary, electrical engineering lecturer and researcher at the Applied Science Faculty of Bethune and Université d'Artois, for the review of this book and the constructive discussions we have had.

My wife, Marina Lainé, for her careful proofreading, her critical approach, her corrections and suggestions and for putting up with my cogitations and insomnias during the months of writing.

Alain Luguet, from *Deobeck Supérieur* editions, for the trust he has put in me and for his advice.

Université d'Artois, and particularly its vice-president Eric Monflier, head of Bethune Applied Science Faculty, Gabriel Vélu, and Jean-Philippe Lecointe, head of the Electrical Engineering Systems and Environment Research laboratory, for their support.

Yves-Pierre Frugier, who translated this book into English.

Author

Bertrand Cassoret is a graduate engineer and PhD in electrical engineering. As a Senior Lecturer at Université d'Artois in France, his research work is partly dedicated to energy efficiency.

Introduction

"How shall we manage when there is no more oil?" I would ask myself that question when I was still a child. "We'll find something else", my mother would answer.

Forty years later, nothing else has yet been found. Our world is even more dependent on fossil energies – coal, gas and oil – which we will obviously miss one day. Yet, a strong environmental awareness has emerged over the last years, particularly in respect to global warming. Renewable energies have definitely been largely developing and waste is more and more fought against. Despite all that, the world's consumption of fossil energies is still increasing: a terrible problem to which there is still no real solution.

I would not claim to be a specialist in environmental issues or to have read or understood everything. But, with a passion for those matters, I have been gathering a lot of documentation for years. My approach finds its way through such subjects as physics, technology, geography, meteorology, history, economics, demography, pollution, health, social organization and the well-being concept... A huge programme! But all this is linked to energy. The topic is so vast that it is hard to get a comprehensive view of all these questions. I am surely not an expert in geology, meteorology, drilling techniques, electrical networks, nuclear or photovoltaic power, energy storage, history, economics, environmental issues, demography or sociology... So, I have read and tried to understand what other people say and write. This book is a synthesis of my readings and reflections.

My aim is neither to criticize renewable energies nor the necessary measures in the field of energy efficiency, but rather to show that they carry so little weight before the extent of the issues. The aim is even less to preach to anyone, to give rise to any guilt or to criticize consumers, a group to which I obviously belong.

I am not writing just for specialists. I hope I am making myself understood to everyone and that the inevitable figures and little calculations will not put some readers off. I hope to add my contribution to the numerous debates and views on energy issues in a rational way.

In order to make sure I am understood, I will immediately reveal the message that I feel is the most important of all: do not be angry at politicians if the situation is deteriorating. They can't go against the laws of physics. This book is pessimistic, and I think it is important to be so. You will be less disappointed when you are expecting the worst. An excessive optimism aimed at showing that there are comfortable solutions to those issues is likely to outrage the people who believe in them and who will naturally think they have been badly governed as they see their living conditions getting worse.

I will thus attempt to:

- Explain the concepts of energy and power.
- Review the consumption of energy in France and around the world: coal, gas, oil, electricity, renewables, primary energy, final energy and the evolution of consumption.

- Show how dependent we are on energy, how important it is, how much it influences the organization of our societies, economic exchanges, employment.
- Scrutinize the numerous issues related to energy: global warming, all sorts of pollution, the depletion of resources.
- Compare the hazards and issues related to the various energy sources.
- Examine the energy resources we may hope to have available.
- Draw the synthesis of a few French energy transition scenarios.
- Show the limits of energy efficiency and sobriety.
- Approach money matters simply.
- Refute a few myths and legends that suggest magic remedies.
- Suggest a few pointers towards solutions.

I will annoy you with formulas, figures and graphs to show you that our way of life is not sustainable. This has been a rather classic speech for a few years which you will have heard before for sure and you are not necessarily willing to hear it again. But my version of it is different as I do not suggest any easy solution to those huge issues. Chin up!

A former edition of this book was written between 2015 and 2017 and was released in French in March 2018. At the beginning of spring 2019, *De Boeck Supérieur* suggested a republication, which was released in October. This is the version that has been translated into English. As compared with the former version, most of the figures and graphs in respect to current affairs have been updated. I have also added a lot of supplementary information the previous version may have missed. My interest in the subject being still so keen and considering the importance of current events, I thought it might be relevant to clarify and complete several sections. The reader will thus find further information about the origin of energy, the evolution of world consumption, the links with global warming, the storage of carbon, the material and area footprints of energy sources, the transition scenarios and pointers to possible solutions. I am well aware that the issues are so complex that it is difficult to be exhaustive, but I hope that I have now provided the reader with as comprehensive an overview as possible of energy transition-related matters.

The names in square brackets [...] refer to the bibliographic references listed at the end of the book.

1 What Is Energy?

The concept of energy is not that simple to approach. Energy is not always visible or palpable. It is hard to quantify. It is not necessarily material, and its existence may even be ignored. Yet, energy is indispensable to life. It is omnipresent in our activities and influences them considerably.

1.1 ENERGY IN RICH COUNTRIES' DAILY LIFE

At night, ventilation devices, internet boxes, freezers, refrigerators, alarm clocks, chargers and various electrical devices left on stand-by consume energy permanently. In the morning, electrical power supplies light. Energy, mostly gas, is required to heat up homes.

Preparing breakfast or other meals requires the consumption of energy: coffee makers, toasters, ovens, microwaves, hotplates, dishwashers, etc.

What about the bathroom? We would not wash so often without abundant energy. You need some to pump water up the water tower, to heat it up and more to make soap.

To listen to the radio, we use electrical appliances which receive waves from electrical emitters, relaying the programmes made in studios which are inconceivable without electrical power. Of course, it is the same with television.

Telephones are charged with electricity. E-mails and internet data are stored on IT servers which are greedy for electricity.

To go to work, most of us need petrol for our cars or electricity for public transport.

In almost all workplaces, there are computers, lighting, heating, ventilation, various electrical appliances and even machines and vehicles running on petroleum or gas.

Anything we buy requires energy to be produced. For any of the things around us, base ores had to be mined – generally with the use of oil-fuelled machines – and transported. Coal, gas, oil and electricity are used to run the transformation and manufacturing factories, and then, all these products have to be transported too.

Anything we eat requires energy. Food is the energy provided to living creatures, but let us not forget about the fuel required by agricultural machinery, the fabrication of fertilizers, the running of food-processing factories, transport systems, etc. We would not eat the same food if fields were ploughed using animal power, if there were no available energy to preserve food or transport it.

Our clothes are often manufactured from oil in energy-greedy factories, and they often have to be transported from thousands of miles away on oil-fuelled ships.

Of course, all the shops from which we purchase these goods also consume energy for their lighting, heating, ventilation, IT equipment, handling and associated offices. And a lot of energy was required to build them to start with.

At the other end of the chain, energy is also required to carry our litter, recycle glass, bury the final waste, depollute water, etc.

Our homes would not be what they are if their foundations had to be dug out by hand rather than with an oil-fuelled excavator, if the building materials had to be transported on muleback rather than on an oil-fuelled truck, if the roof timbers had to be built by hand rather than in energy-greedy factories, if there had not been kilns to fire the bricks.

We are lucky to get healthcare when necessary. Prescribed medicines, corrective lenses, dental prostheses, etc., are easily made available thanks to energy-hungry machines and transport systems. Hospitals, which consume a lot of energy, are there for us in case of more serious health issues: ventilation, lighting, heating, cleaning, disinfection processes, refrigeration, medical equipment of all sorts, operating theatres, etc., are not run on thin air.

Many of us have leisure activities. We would not go to the swimming pool so often if the water was not heated. Bikes, sport shoes, rackets, balls, work-out equipment, etc., are all made thanks to some energy. We even frequently use our car to go and do some sport. Cinemas, concert halls, gyms and museums also consume energy for their ventilation, lighting, heating, etc. Sport events and shows would be unimaginable without a lot of energy. We need some for the construction of stadiums and halls, their heating, lighting and ventilation, to transport their equipment, to bring players and artists, to take the public to events, to carry out the promotion of events. Even the Tour de France, though a bicycle race, is a big oil consumer, given the number of follower vehicles.

Many of us go on holiday, but rarely by bicycle. The energy required to build blocks of flats, villas, hotels, restaurants, casinos, seawalls, amusement parks, ski lifts, sport centres, museums was considerable. Huge amounts of energy are required for the running of all these installations, and to clean beaches, to operate carousels, cable cars, ships or rescue helicopters, etc.

Some people travel by train, which is less energy-greedy than cars, but railways are still very big electrical power consumers. Airplanes are big oil consumers. Of course, the manufacturing of those means of transport is a high energy-consuming process, particularly for the production of steel.

Many people are careful with their consumption of energy: they use low-energy bulbs, they drive more calmly or even walk, they switch off devices instead of keeping them on stand-by, they carefully adjust heating settings. But all that does not account for much, compared to the rest.

Other people, scarce as they may be, and often belonging to the less well-off, behave more virtuously: no car, no holidays, no telephone, etc. Their consumption is slightly lower, but they are still very dependent on energy to move around – even when using public transport – to cook their food, use hot water, live in their own home, get healthcare, etc.

Three-quarters of French wage-earners work for service industries and are paid for managing finance, administering, providing healthcare or assistance, communicating, teaching, doing research, selling, organizing, developing products, etc. Goods and properties are more and more abundant while there are fewer and fewer people to manufacture them. Food is abundant while less than 3% of the working population work in the agriculture sector. And all this would just not work without high energy-consuming machines, factories or transport systems. The organization of society relies entirely on abundant energy. The only people living with really low energy consumption are those in poor countries who eat what they grow, live in rudimentary housing, get little healthcare, do not travel much and have limited access to culture and leisure. Their lifestyle, which they generally endeavour to improve, is similar to the one the French used to have at the beginning of the 19th century.

1.2 THE LAWS OF PHYSICS

Energy is what is used to transform our environment, to create movement, radiation, electrical currents, chemical reactions, to produce heat along with every process. Energy is therefore required to move a mass or to deform it, to supply light or create electromagnetic waves, to operate our numerous electrical appliances, to create the chemical processes that are essential to life, to keep us warm.

Photosynthesis, for example, is a chemical reaction through which plants transform solar energy into an organic matter containing nutritional calories. Our muscles can then transform that energy into movements that can operate pedals driving a dynamo producing electricity to generate light and heat.

Two fundamental laws are permanently true in the field of energy, until proven otherwise:

- **Energy conservation**: "I believe in life after death, just because energy cannot die. It travels, transforms, but never stands still", Albert Einstein is said to have declared.

  The amount of energy that is put out by a system is equal to the amount put into it. **Thus, energy can only be transformed but not be created.** Energy cannot appear miraculously! For example: a power station, which transforms gas into electricity, will give back exactly the same amount of electrical energy and heat as the energy it has consumed in the form of gas. Heat results from inevitable losses. The amount of usable energy put out as electricity is thus necessarily lower than that put in, in the form of gas.

  Solar energy is another example: the sun sends a certain amount of energy over a one-square-metre surface area, each year – about 1,300 kWh in France. It is therefore impossible to extract more than that from a solar panel, no matter how sophisticated it may be.
- **Increases in entropy**: The quality of energy always degrades itself from the concentrated to the dispersed, from order to disorder. A power station using gas – concentrated energy – transforms part of it into heat, which will disperse. It creates electricity, which will also turn into heat in the course of its distribution, and will then disperse: electric wires will slightly heat up, and so will electric appliances. Even a fan, which is meant to cool people, will also create some friction resulting in heat, which will disperse in the atmosphere and eventually vanish into space. A fan consumes energy, thus

increasing the temperature of the room where it is installed, even if you can feel the coolness of its air flow. Another example: a motor-car transforms the energy stored in its petrol tank into heat – the engine gets hot – and into movement, which is what it is meant to produce, but movement creates friction, particularly the friction of the car body travelling through the air, which eventually results in heat.

In the solar system, energy is mainly concentrated in the sun and disperses permanently. The energy consumed always transforms into heat, which disperses.

So, two systems consuming the same amount of energy will heat up equally. A refrigerator, which is meant to produce coolness, gets as warm as any appliance consuming the same amount of energy (its rear plate gets warm). Ten TV-sets consuming 100 watts each get collectively as warm as a radiator consuming 1,000 watts. A top-range radiator is sometimes thought to consume less electricity than a cheaper one. It is only partially true. The distribution of heat, as well as the diffusion mode, have an influence on comfort but two radiators consuming the same amount of energy produce exactly the same amount of heat.

1.3   WHERE DOES ENERGY COME FROM?

A huge amount of energy has been present across the universe since its origin. Where does it come from? This is a vast question to which I would not claim to have an answer. Energy is present in two forms: the nuclear energy contained in any matter, and the kinetic energy of the movement of stars or of other particles moving through space.

Figure 1.1 is meant to summarize all this, though not comprehensively.

- Atoms, which constitute all matter, hold a huge amount of energy in proportion to their mass. Nuclear power stations and the sun exploit this energy, but we often forget that part of the heat in the centre of the Earth results from nuclear reactions, which allow for deep geothermal systems.
- In the sun, a colossal amount of nuclear fusion reactions (400 million billion billion watts!) creates intense electromagnetic radiation. Our planet picks up a small share of this radiation through which it is heated. Part of this heat contributes to maintaining the temperature of the shallow underground, resulting in certain forms of geothermal energy. Photovoltaic panels transform the solar radiation into electricity. Solar radiation allows for photosynthesis, which enables plants (biomass) to grow, thus making life possible. The transformation of organic materials resulting from life produced fossil energies (petroleum, gas, coal) which therefore originate from solar energy. The sun allows for the evaporation of water resulting in rain and rivers and eventually in hydropower. As air masses are heated up by the sun, they are set in motion, creating wind and eventually wind-power.

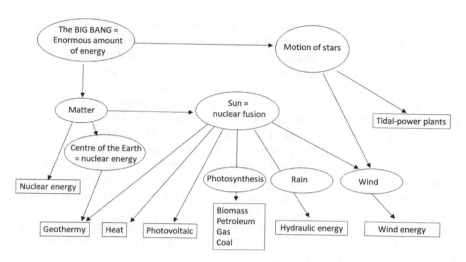

FIGURE 1.1   Origin of energy on Earth.

- The gravitational pull of the moon revolving around the Earth creates tides, allowing for the production of energy by tidal power-plants, which accounts for a very small share of our electricity. Part of the wind is due to the rotation of planet Earth on its own axis.

All the existing sorts of energy do not appear in Figure 1.1; some types of ocean energy in particular are not mentioned.

1.4   ENERGY AND POWER

Energy is often confused with power. Power is generally measured in watts, or, commonly, in horsepower for oil-fuelled engines, 1 horsepower corresponding to 736 watts.

Power is related to a diffusion of energy through – for example – visible rays, electric cables, a rotating drive chain or belt, a rope being pulled on, a radiator diffusing heat, etc.

An amount of energy may, for example, be a litre of petrol, a woodpile, a gas tank, a pile of coal, a mass held high up, a mass in motion, a plate of French fries.

Electric meters count energy in watts per hour, gas meters count energy in cubic metres, petrol stations count energy in litres or gallons of petrol and lumberjacks count energy in cubic metres of logs.

Power is an amount of energy per unit of time: *power = energy/time*. A petrol tank is a reserve of energy, while the number of litres of petrol consumed per hour corresponds to the average power consumed. Inversely, to find the amount of energy you just need to multiply power by time. Thus, an appliance consuming a power of 1,000 watts for two hours will have consumed an amount of energy of 2,000 watt-hours (Wh). This is the amount you are generally invoiced for.

Careful! We are speaking here about watts multiplied by hours, i.e. watt-hours (Wh) and not watts per hour (W/h). It is very common to see articles, even in reputed newspapers, mentioning watts per hour, which does not mean the same thing at all, and has the annoying knack of irritating me. It is common for journalists to speak about consumption in watts per year, which does not mean anything. They should say or write "watt-hours per year". An electric vehicle consumes about 15 kWh (15 kilowatt-hours = 15,000 watt-hours) to cover 60 miles, in the same way as a petrol vehicle consumes around 6 litres to cover 60 miles (47 miles to the gallon).

When wind-turbines, solar panels or nuclear plants are installed, the specialists refer to the installed power in watts, which gives the maximum power that these systems will be able to produce in the form of electricity at a given time. That power depends upon the strength of the wind at all times for wind-turbines and upon the amount of sunshine for solar panels. The amount of energy supplied each year is calculated by multiplying the average power delivered – depending on weather conditions – by the number of hours in a year. There is often confusion between the power installed and the energy produced.

Several units are used to count energy and we can easily skip from one to the other through a simple multiplication or division. Watt-hours are commonly used for electricity, while the energy contained in food is usually expressed in calories. But an amount of electricity could as well be expressed in calories and the energy contained in a plate of chips in watt-hours.

The typical unit for physicists is the joule, which is used in the international system of units (SI) in the equations of physics.

The ton oil equivalent (toe) corresponds to the average energy provided by one ton of crude oil. It is used by economists because it is easier to use to calculate larger amounts.

The electron volt (eV) is, on the opposite scale, easier for the expression of small amounts, particularly for the energy of electrons.

The British invented the British thermal unit (Btu) which is adapted to degrees Fahrenheit.

Other units are used in everyday life in a less official manner: the litre or gallon of petrol (1 litre = about 10 kWh, i.e. 10,000 Wh), the cubic metre of logs (1,500 to 2,000 kWh), the bag of charcoal, the gas tank, the electric battery, etc.

See below the equivalences between the various energy units:

1 joule (J) = 1 watt-second (Ws)
1 watt-hour (Wh) = 3,600 joules (J) = 860.11 calories
1 calorie = 4.1855 J (amount of energy required to raise the temperature of one
    gram of water by one degree Celsius)
1 ton oil equivalent (toe) = 11,630 kWh = 7.33 oil drums
1 electron volt (eV) = 1.602×10^{-19} J
1 Btu = 1,055 J

A petrol-fuelled vehicle running for 2 hours and doing 47 miles to the gallon will consume 12 litres (2.64 imp. gallons), i.e. an amount of energy of around 120 kWh or

120,000 Wh. The average power consumed is obtained by dividing energy by time (2 hours): 120,000/2 = 60,000 watts. Given that one horsepower is worth 736 W, this power can be expressed as: 60,000/736 = 81 hp. This is the average power consumed by the vehicle thanks to petrol, which is far higher than the one returned by the driving wheels because of losses.

1.5 ENERGY STORAGE

The storage of energy is often a difficult process. For example, when a spring is compressed, the energy it has been provided with is stored so long as it is compressed. Of course, the only thing the spring wants is to unwind.

Energy does not like to be stored or concentrated. It is in its nature to try to disperse. Storing energy is often dangerous: a petrol or a gas tank may explode to release energy, a mass held high up may fall, a woodpile may catch fire, a dam may give way, an inflated balloon may burst, etc.

Moreover, as energy is obtained by multiplying power by time and since it cannot be infinite, the storage or release of energy necessarily takes time. A real hindrance to the development of electric vehicles, for example, is that, even if available batteries could store a lot of energy in a short time, the problem would then come from the power grid which would find it difficult to provide for the necessary power requirements.

There is as much energy (around 10 kWh or 10,000 Wh) in:

- 0.5 mg of uranium 235
- 1 litre of petrol (petroleum)
- 1.5 kg of coal
- 2.5 kg of dry wood
- 10.7 kg of potatoes
- A 250-kg lead battery or a 60-kg lithium battery

By comparing the examples of orders of magnitude above, we observe that petrol allows for a high concentration of energy, not mentioning uranium nuclear reactions. A litre of petrol, the weight of which is not more than about 750 g, contains as much energy as a 250-kg lead battery! Putting a motor car into motion requires a reserve of energy upon which autonomy relies directly. Even if more efficient batteries, such as lithium, exist, it is hard for an electric vehicle running on batteries to compete with the autonomy of a petrol-fuelled vehicle. It will be difficult to find as convenient an energy storage for a car as a petrol tank. Crude oil is a very concentrated, stable (not so explosive) and rather user-friendly energy.

Some navy submarines run on nuclear propulsion: the energy density of the uranium used provides a huge autonomy, which is strategically of major importance.

A typical French baguette contains about 700 kilocalories (kcal). The brave could verify that they would have to eat 12 of them to get as much energy as there is in 1 litre of crude oil!

1.6 ORDERS OF MAGNITUDE

One kWh (kilowatt-hour) roughly represents the amount of energy provided by 3 m² of photovoltaic solar panels in one average day in France. This amount of energy corresponds to less than a 7-km distance (4.35 miles) travelled by an electric car, to 100 hours of a 10-W LED light bulb, to 5–10 hours of use of a TV set, to 1 hour of use of a 1,000-W microwave, to half an hour of heating with a 2,000-W radiator, to less than a 5-minute shower, if hot of course!

A typical French household consumes an average of 3,000 kWh of specific electricity (i.e. except heating and hot water). With 24 hours in a day and 365 days in a year, it accounts for a permanent use of power of 3,000,000/(24 × 365) = 342 W.

If we include heating, an average home in France consumes 18,000 kWh per year, i.e. an average power of 18,000,000/(24 × 365) = 2,054 W permanently, which corresponds to a large electric radiator that would be working at maximum, 24/7 throughout the year. It is just enormous!

An elite athlete, e.g. Christopher Froome, can supply a power of over 1,000 W when climbing Alpe d'Huez, but not for more than a few seconds. In half an hour, an elite athlete is able to supply an average power of less than 500 W.

A human being eating a standard amount of 2,100 kcal per day (i.e. 2,400 Wh per day), will not be able to supply, physically, more than 2,400/24 = 100 W permanently. Actually, as the energy we eat is mainly dispersed in heat, supplying 80 W in the form of movement throughout an eight-hour working day – i.e. a ridiculous energy of 640 W = 0.64 kWh – represents a serious amount of physical work for a human being.

The average annual consumption of a French home – 18,000 kWh – accounts for the equivalent of 18,000/0.64 = 28,125 busy working days! As a year has 365 days, we would need 28,125/365 = 77 persons, pedalling for 8 hours every day – even on Sundays – to operate a perfect system with no energy loss, to heat up an average

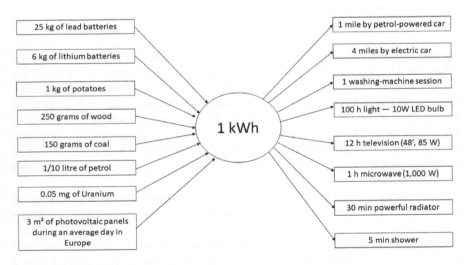

FIGURE 1.2 Production, storage and consumption of 1 kWh.

home, supply hot water and operate the electrical household appliances! And this comes without accounting for what the inhabitants of this home would spend to move around, eat, dress and equip themselves.

If pedalling for 150 hours per month (i.e. a standard working period in France), a worker supplying 80 W on average would thus supply around $150 \times 80 = 12,000$ kWh, i.e. just over 1 litre of petrol for which we paid less than €2 in 2019!

Having a human being pedal for a €1,500 monthly salary – which is too low considering charges! – to produce 12 kWh/month with a no-loss system, would set the price of a kWh at over €125, i.e. 1,000 times the price of electricity or petrol! Keep that in mind next time you fill up: your 50-litre (11-imp. gallons) petrol tank represents more than 40 months of human pedalling!

According to Jean-Marc Jancovici [Jancovici Web], a French specialist in these matters who has hugely inspired me, an average French person has the energy equivalent of about 500 human beings at their disposal if we take food, consumer goods, transport and dwelling into account. Jean-Marc Jancovici points out that the end of slavery must have been made easier through the simple fact that paying for machinery energy had become cheaper than feeding a slave. Jean-François Mouhot, a historian, wrote:

> The new use of steam power was probably a necessary condition for the abolition of slavery. The exploitation of fossil energies resulted in an energy transition which made slavery more and more superfluous, machines consequently replacing forced labour in modern societies *de facto*.
>
> **[Mouhot]**

Supplying a slave with only €4 of food daily nowadays for a supply of 100 W every 10 hours each day, i.e. 1 kWh per day – how exhausting! – would bring the price of 1 kWh to €4, which would be about 27 times the price of 1 kWh supplied by the French public grid in 2019!

2 Energy Consumption in France and across the World

2.1 ENERGIES OF ALL KINDS

A distinction is to be made between primary, secondary, final and useful energy consumptions. For electricity, it is even referred to gross and net consumptions, including or not the electricity consumption of the production systems. These concepts may complicate people's understanding and result in some disputed values.

Primary energy refers to the energy available before any transformation. It may be coal, gas, petroleum, uranium, wind, solar rays, wood, hot water springs etc. They are energy sources available in nature.

Final energy is the energy used by consumers. It can be a litre of refined petrol contained in a car tank, or an electrical kWh operating a washing machine. It is the energy consumers pay for. As energy is used to extract, refine, cut out, exploit and transport petrol, gas, coal or wood, and because there is a loss during production processes and transport, the amount of final energy is smaller than that of primary energy. Yet, the most important difference between primary and final energy turns out to be with electricity. As electricity is not a primary energy source since there is none in nature, it is not listed among primary energies. Electricity can be produced from coal, gas, crude oil, wood, renewables or nuclear energy etc. it is thus considered a final energy. It is the same for heat networks distributing heat to various users through hot water or steam circulating in pipes; they belong to the final energy category. In France, the consumption of primary energy in 2018 was about 3,000 TWh (1 TWh = 1 terawatt-hour = 10^{12} Wh = 1 million million Wh) while the amount of final energy consumed was 1,800 TWh (or 253.5 and 150.3 Mtoe) [Datalab énergie], i.e. quite a large difference of 40%.

Secondary energy is not so often referred to. It stands in between primary and final energies. For example, it may include the electricity put out by power stations, the amount of which is lower than primary energy because of a loss due to production processes, but higher than final energy because of a loss due to transport.

Useful energy can also be referred to. Just a small part of the energy consumers pay for is really useful, due to losses. For example, a light bulb does not transform the whole electrical energy consumed into light. Likewise, a car engine does not transform the whole petrol energy consumed into motion because an inevitable loss occurs due to the energy more directly transformed into heat. Figure 2.1 summarizes this issue. Eventually, a small part of the primary energy is useful. Even with a

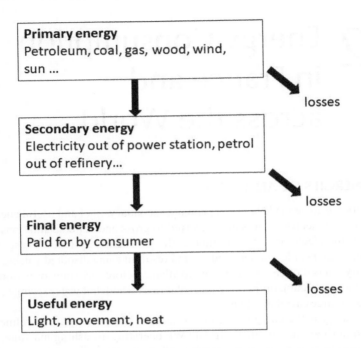

Primary energy
Petroleum, coal, gas, wood, wind,
sun ...

losses

Secondary energy
Electricity out of power station, petrol
out of refinery...

losses

Final energy
Paid for by consumer

losses

Useful energy
Light, movement, heat

FIGURE 2.1   Primary, secondary, final and useful energies.

high-performance petrol engine, even with high-performance LED bulbs, less than 20% of the primary energy is converted into motion or light. The reduction of losses everyone would hope for is made difficult by the laws of physics.

Figures 2.2 and 2.3 give an idea of the distribution of energy consumption in France and across the world.

Figure 2.2 shows that more than 80% of the world's primary energy is of fossil origin, i.e. from crude oil, gas or coal. Crude oil is the world's main energy source, coal following close behind and then gas. "Of fossil origin" means that it took these energy sources millions of years to form and that they will inevitably run out one day. One may wonder when, but the depletion will occur, for sure.

Renewable energy accounts for 14% of the world's primary energy. Wood comes first at around 10%. It is the world's number one renewable energy. Then comes hydraulic energy, at around 3%. Wind and solar energy currently play a very small part despite their large media coverage: less than 2% for both combined [IEA].

Around 19% of the world's final energy is consumed in the form of electricity.

The situation in France is rather peculiar since nuclear is the leading primary energy supplying electricity. As a consequence, while being the world's leading energy source producing electricity, coal is used very little in this country and so is gas. France has invested a lot in nuclear energy. Therefore, electricity is logically much more used here than anywhere else: 25% of the final energy, as opposed to 19% in the rest of the world. Electric heating, in particular, is very popular in France. Obviously, nuclear energy opponents are not happy with this situation, but, as we'll

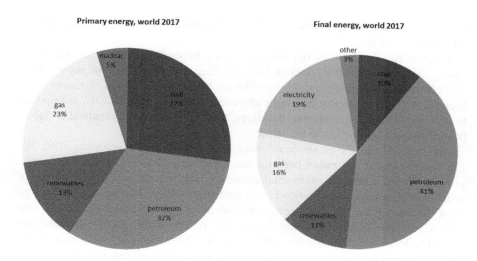

FIGURE 2.2 Distribution of primary and final energy in the world in 2017. (Source: European Commission [EU Energy].)

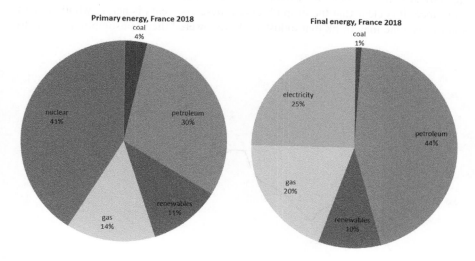

FIGURE 2.3 Distribution of primary and final energy consumption in France in 2018. (Source: *Commissariat général au développement durable, Ministère de la Transition Ecologique et Solidaire* [Datalab énergie].)

see later on, air-polluting emissions are lower in France than in other comparable countries.

This being said, France, like other countries, is very dependent on fossil energies. Renewables account for 11% of the French primary energy consumption and for 16% of final energy, mainly with wood and hydro-energy. Wind energy, though heavily

covered in the media, accounted for 1.5% of the final energy in 2018, and photovoltaic energy even less.

Final energy consumption in France is first due to residential and office buildings,
which absorb around 46% [Datalab énergie]. Transport systems come second with
32%, while industry, the importance of which has largely declined in recent years
because of factory closures, no longer absorbed more than 19% in 2017, as opposed
to 25% in 2000. With residential buildings, 80% of the energy consumed is due to
heating and the production of hot water.

Figure 2.4 shows the evolution of energy consumption in France since 1965. We
can observe that it has rather been decreasing after a period of strong continuous
growth. Would a new environmental awareness and the measures taken in recent
years to limit energy consumption have a significant effect? Maybe, but if things go
on at the same pace, we shall remain dependent on fossil energies for quite a long
time. Upon consideration, in France as in other rich countries, energy consumption
started to decrease just before the 2008 crisis. One should probably see here a cause–
effect relationship. The crisis then led to a slight drop in consumption and the economy has never fully restarted since. In fact, the decline of industries was the main
reason for lower energy consumption in France. It was down by 20% between 2000
and 2017. Figure 2.5 shows the evolution of the various fields for energy consumption
in France. It is clear that the drop observed these last years is nearly wholly due to
industries. One may think that industries have lowered their consumption thanks to

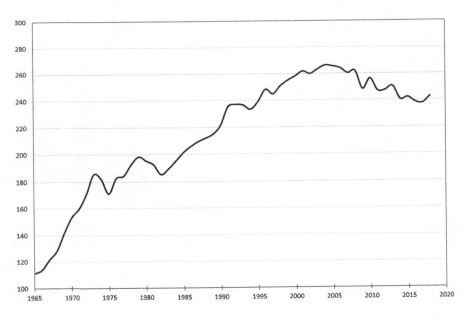

FIGURE 2.4 Evolution of France's consumption in primary energy since 1965, in millions
of ton of oil equivalent. (Source: *BP statistical review of world energy*, 2019.)

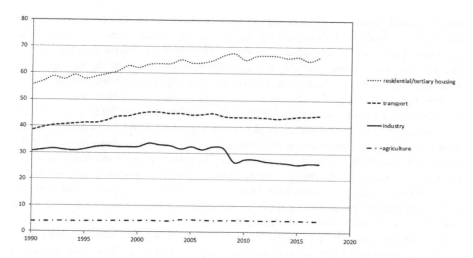

FIGURE 2.5 Seasonally adjusted evolution of final energy consumption per sector in France from 1990 to 2017, in millions of ton of oil equivalent. (Source: *Ministère de la Transition Écologique et Solidaire*, September 2019.)

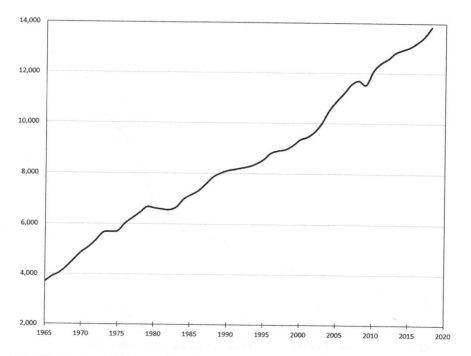

FIGURE 2.6 Evolution of the world's primary energy consumption since 1965, in millions of ton of oil equivalent. (Source: *BP statistical review of world energy*, 2019.)

more efficient systems, but the numerous factory closures cannot be ignored. France has been gradually deindustrializing but we are not buying fewer manufactured products. These are simply made elsewhere. Therefore, our impact on the world's energy consumption has probably not decreased, not to mention the fact that outsourcing operations obviously require large amounts of crude oil due to transport.

The most worrying observation is shown by Figure 2.6 which illustrates the world's energy consumption since 1965. After a slight drop in 2008, it has clearly gone up again. This rise is mostly explained in Figures 2.7 and 2.8, which show the evolution of energy consumption in China and India, with their sharp increase at the very beginning of this century. There certainly lies the reason for the stabilization of the richer countries' consumption, many of their goods being now manufactured in Asia, and particularly in China. In 2018, China consumed 23% of the world's energy. It is said to have opened one coal power station every week from 2005 to 2014, in order to meet its electricity requirements!

On average, from 2001 to 2018, the increase of the world's annual energy consumption accounted for more than the consumption in France. Likewise, the extra amount of electricity consumed each year across the world is higher than the French electric consumption! **More than one France is to be added each year!**

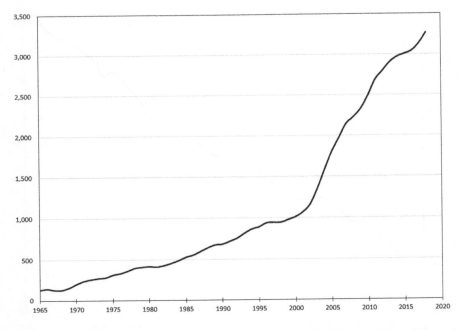

FIGURE 2.7 Evolution of China's primary energy consumption since 1965, in millions of ton of oil equivalent. (Source: *BP statistical review of world energy*, 2019.)

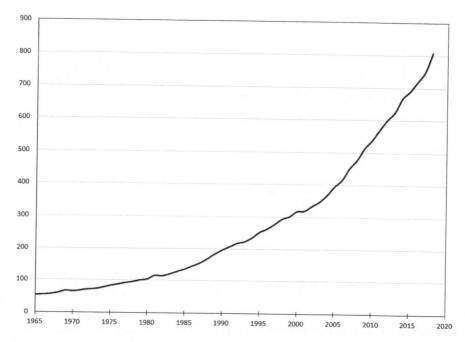

FIGURE 2.8 Evolution of India's primary energy consumption since 1965, in millions of ton of oil equivalent. (Source: *BP statistical review of world energy*, 2019.)

2.2 ELECTRICITY PRODUCTION

Electricity only accounts for 19% of the world's final energy and less than a quarter of that of France. However, it holds a considerable place in media coverage since it can be produced from various energy sources such as coal (very polluting), nuclear energy (impressive) or wind (more fashionable). It is consequently at the heart of many debates. For some people, "energy transition" goes hand in hand with "electric transition". One may remember the argument that took place between the two rounds of the 2007 presidential election in France. Ségolène Royal, the left-wing candidate, attacked Nicolas Sarkozy, right wing, saying that nuclear only accounted for 17% of the electric power produced while her rival was rather inclined to set it at 50%. Actually, nuclear energy accounted for 78% of our electricity but 17% of our energy at the time.

The world's leading energy source for the production of electricity is also the most polluting: coal, followed by gas (see Figure 2.10). But electricity can also be produced thanks to non-fossil sources: renewables (hydro-power, wind, solar, wood, biogas etc.) or nuclear. The part played by electricity is therefore likely to increase in the future when crude oil or gas depletion becomes a problem for the running of vehicles or the production of heat.

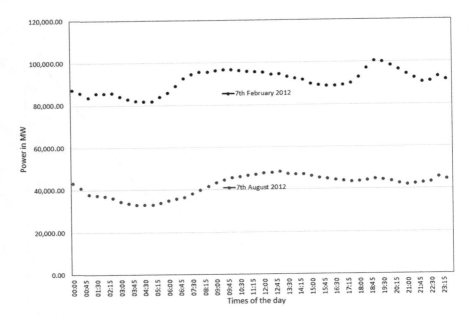

FIGURE 2.9 Power electrically consumed in France during February 7 and August 7, 2012. (Source: RTE.)

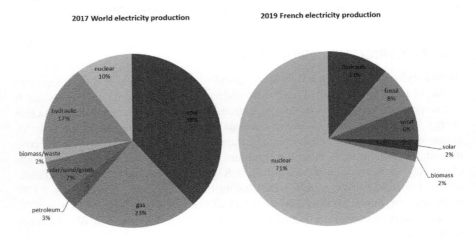

FIGURE 2.10 Production of electricity across the world in 2017 and in France in 2019. (Sources: International Energy Agency, RTE.)

An essential and problematic characteristic of electricity is that it is very difficult to store while its production is very irregular. We consume more of it in winter than in summer, particularly to get warmth and light. Its consumption also varies a lot during the day. See Figure 2.9 from RTE's website (RTE: the company managing the

French grid) illustrating the demand set up in France during one cold day (February 7, 2012, a day of record power consumption) and during one warm day (August 7, 2012). The scales are the same for both days.

The observation is clear: the power consumed varies all the time throughout the day and throughout the year, from 33,007 MW to more than 100,000 MW according to these two examples. Considering the low possible storage capacity, production has to adapt to consumption all the time.

We normally expect an appliance to work when switched on. However, it implies that a power station has to be able to produce the required electricity at any time. As a consequence, production processes have to be adapted all the time, which means power stations have to adjust, restart or shut down. To make the balance between supply and demand easier, many international interconnections exist and allow for some sort of solidarity between countries. They sell and buy from and to one another all the time, according to consumption and production capacities.

Debate sometimes arises between pro- and anti-nuclear groups on this subject, the former claiming that France sells electricity thanks to nuclear, the latter claiming that France is not able to be autonomous despite its nuclear power stations. They are both right. France happens to import electricity, but, on average, it exports more than it imports. And if imports were to be a problem, the conclusion would be that more power stations would be needed.

The general interest is to reduce consumption peaks as they impose the size of installations (power stations, power grids etc.). The best solution would be to have consumption that would be equally distributed over time. This has led to the creation of an off-peak time principle which is an incentive to consume electricity preferably during the night, when the demand set up is low. It is true that electric heating implies high power requirements, but all heating systems have their drawbacks. In order to limit peaks, big consumers, e.g. industries, are required to agree on temporary selective power shutdowns, i.e. to accept to stop consuming energy during those periods.

In France, most electricity is produced by nuclear power stations. In 2019, 71% of electricity was supplied by nuclear, as opposed to 11% by hydro-power, 7% by gas power stations, 6% by wind turbines, under 2% by solar panels and 0.3% by coal power stations (see Figure 2.10). The significant progression of wind and photovoltaic power systems over the last few years is under debate. These energies are symbols for energy transition, green growth and sustainable development. Their contribution so far is very low, but they are progressing quickly. They are renewable and do not emit any pollution when they work, which are two great assets. Their main problem comes from their intermittence and irregularity: their production relies on wind for wind turbines, on the amount of sunshine for photovoltaic panels, which are factors we do not control. Therefore, their production is not controllable, as opposed to other energy production means.

While we are used to adapting production to consumption permanently, thanks to controllable nuclear, gas, coal, fuel-oil, hydraulic production stations, we are installing wind-power and solar systems, the production of energy from which relies on weather conditions. This means that, for the time being, the other power stations have to be able to adapt even more, to produce less when the wind blows more or the sun shines more brightly, or to produce more when wind or sun fail to be present. Wind turbines and photovoltaic panels do not currently replace the other systems but, moreover, the latter, which are used less, still have to exist. For example, in Germany, on September 22, 2017, at 7:30 p.m., while the consumption was 63 MW, the solar production was nil, wind production was only 0.61 GW, i.e. 1.16% of the 52 GW of installed power. As a consequence, the country was eventually supplied by the coal, nuclear, gas, wood and hydraulic controllable production systems. In France, part of the nuclear production could be replaced by further developing wind energy, but this would not mean that a proportional number of nuclear reactors could be shut down.

As any human construction, whether being constructed, maintained or dismantled, results in an environmental impact, one should wonder about the ecological benefit of all extra production means.

Right now, wind turbines have a beneficial role in countries where electricity is produced from fossil energies as these are consequently less used, which reduces their polluting emissions. In France, wind and photovoltaic systems result in a slightly lower production of nuclear waste but with very little participation in the fight against global warming or air pollution to which nuclear has very little contribution. The means invested in these energies might be of better use in other fields, such as home insulation, for example.

The logic presiding over the uncontrollable production systems reaches some limits, and we understand that it will be hardly possible to increase the share of wind or solar electricity without either developing storage solutions or a more important adaptation, not of supply to demand, but of demand to supply, mainly by rescheduling some of the consumption seen as not being priorities.

The storage of electricity can mainly be achieved in three indirect ways.

- The most commonly used system is in a hydraulic form. Water is pumped upward during off-peak hours when electricity is available, whether produced by nuclear or by wind farms, for example, and that water is then released in peak hours, its drop driving turbines producing electricity. This type of storage requires large water reservoirs and/or a big difference in altitude between two reservoirs. This process is used with production dams or with systems called *station de transfert d'énergie par pompage*/pumped energy transfer station (STEP) which are only used for storage. The development of intermittent energies – wind and solar – could therefore be associated with the development of STEPs. In France, although these installations have been widely developed, the total storage capacity accounts for about the consumption of electricity for two hours! Colossal projects are being suggested, such as the creation of sea-water artificial lakes on top of cliffs in Normandy, with the sea as the lower reservoir, a tunnel between the lake and the sea for the water to be pumped upwards or released downwards. Such installations would obviously have an environmental impact. If we consider the opposition faced by the dam in Sivens, it may well be difficult to envisage the construction of many STEPs in the future as the storage of large amounts of energy necessarily requires large artificial lakes.

- Another system consists of the chemical storage in batteries. The amounts of energy stored are low when compared to the size of the batteries, the environmental impact of which is questionable. Progress in the field of batteries is slow, as shown by the history of the electric automobile: the first automobile able to reach a 60-mph speed was electric (*La Jamais contente*, in 1899). Peugeot commercialized an electric vehicle as early as in 1942 and their electric 106 model in 1996. The main problem faced by these cars remains their autonomy, with heavy and bulky batteries for a comparatively small energy storage capacity. As confirmed by the French Academy of Sciences in April 2017, the storage of the energy required by the French consumption of electricity in two days, "using the efficient lithium-ion technologies in use in Tesla motor cars, would require no less than two billion tons of batteries made of 3,600,000 tons of lithium, while 40,000 tons of this metal are mined each year". In Australia, the world's biggest battery, which was inaugurated in 2017, takes up a surface area larger than a football pitch. Combined with wind turbines, it finds its use in absorbing or supplying power over short periods, but its 129-MWh capacity represents less than 20 seconds of the average consumption in Australia and around 9 seconds of the French consumption!

Battery storage is currently envisaged for short periods of time, such as for a supply of electricity in the evening, but not for storing summer energy to be used in winter.

- The third electricity storage principle consists in transforming it into gas. Hydrogen or methane can be produced through electricity. This is the so-called "power to gas" technology. Hydrogen and methane can first be injected into the gas network to then be used to produce electricity, though with heavy losses between the used and the returned electricity, or for other uses. On paper, this technique is the one with the best future. Yet, it is just in its experimental stage and will require the implementation of new infrastructures. Etienne Beeker, a scientific counsellor in charge of energy issues at *France Strategie*, wrote in 2014 that "methanation has no future on a predictable horizon", and that, concerning the production of electricity from hydrogen, "its low yields and high cost will not let it compete with hydraulic pumped energy stations or electrochemical batteries before long." [Beeker]

Other storage methods can be used, such as compressed air. But these types of storage do not seem to be considered on a large scale, as far as I know. Steven Chu, the 1997 physics Nobel Prize winner and Barack Obama's energy secretary between 2009 and 2013, said, in 2019: "I do not think that it is possible to reach 100% renewable energies in the near future. We do not have enough electricity storage solutions" [CHU]

Therefore, the development of wind and solar energy will probably not imply just a supply-to-demand but also a demand-to-supply adaptation. This is part of the role of the so-called "smart grids". Some appliances that are not seen as a priority could be shut down when production systems are inadequate. One may imagine a pricing of electricity fluctuating according to the amount of wind or of sunlight and to the consumption called for, using appliances with a capacity to schedule their consumption on the basis of changing prices and the level of priority granted to each of them. Smart electricity meters will help. This evolution will have little impact if the use of washing machines or dishwashers is to be slightly rescheduled, but it is a trend that is to lead to lower comfort. What shall our reaction be like if electricity becomes very expensive when it's time to cook our meals or to warm up the bathroom with extra heating devices? How shall we organize our society if we have to reschedule the timing of factories' or bakers' work, TGV timetables, nocturnal football matches or performances?

Wind turbines and solar panels are often considered as local production systems, close to consumers, avoiding losses in long power lines and helping to do without large energy businesses. Yet, the argument put forward by their promoters with respect to the intermittence of wind and sunlight is geographical smoothing. When the wind does not blow in some areas, it may blow elsewhere. The sun does not set at the same time everywhere. Wind turbines in the northern areas could thus supply the south where and when the wind is inadequate, and vice versa, the same with western region solar panels and eastern areas. This way of reasoning is most questionable, as there are times, particularly in the evening, when the sun has set and the wind is low all over Europe. A PhD thesis dealing with "meteorological and climatic potentials and limits of the smoothing of renewable energies" explains that

> in spite of the very large area covered by the European continent, the spatial smoothing of production capacities and a broad integration of the network, low-wind and resulting low-production episodes remain. These meteorological situations show the limits of a smoothing of renewable energy.
>
> **[Lassonde]**

Besides, the smoothing argument clearly shows that these means of production are anything but local. It is obvious today that wind turbines generate more exchanges of electricity between regions and countries and the resulting construction of more high-voltage electric lines. "The more renewable energies in the mix, the higher the needed interconnexion capacities", says a report produced by the company in charge of the French electricity transmission network (RTE). The construction of these very often faces strong opposition.

Resorting to gas is a danger for the future. By shutting down nuclear reactors that we hope to replace with non-powered renewables, painful postponements of consumption and storage that is complex to set up, we run the risk of power cuts. As a response to the discontent it would create, one may fear that gas power stations, so easy to build, would be constructed in a hurry in spite of their emissions of CO_2

and other pollutants, and the fact they would make us even more dependent on our gas suppliers. In their 2017 budget estimate, RTE explains that "depending on configurations, the development of gas power stations may … result from the need of spare solutions to compensate for the intermittence of renewable energies" [RTE BP 2017]. By the way, in France where the nuclear power station of Fessenheim is being shut down, the decision to build a new gas power station in Landivisiau (Britanny) has been taken.

According to some people, all our evils stem from the centralization of our electricity production means, while the safe solution would be the installation of many small decentralized units. "Local is beautiful"! The local option is yet relativized by the necessary interconnections I have just mentioned. Besides, the environmental impact of just one large installation is lower than the one of ten installations ten times less powerful. Indeed, the yield of a big machine is always higher than the yield of a smaller one and requires proportionally less material to be built.

Some electricity companies sell electricity reputed to be produced by renewable energies only. I consider this is close to a misleading advertising message, primarily because electricity corresponds to a flow of electrons mixing in the interconnected cables. Imagine a river fed by several tributaries and from which some people would pump water, claiming that it comes from one of the tributaries only. Moreover, these companies actually purchase, each year, as much electricity from renewables as they sell, but not in real time. The power called for by consumers is very often higher than the production capacity of renewables. It is therefore wrong to think that one does not consume any nuclear or fossil electricity just because one's supplier is said to sell green electricity.

The only way to be sure to consume local renewable electricity would be to have no connection with the grid and to store one's own. But, considering how difficult the storage is, this type of installation is currently not compatible with typical consumption. Some mountain huts are not connected to the electric grid and store their solar-panel electricity in batteries. They manage to get some light for a few hours in the evening but would absolutely not be able to supply a washing machine, TV sets, computers, hotplates, ovens or coffee makers etc. By the way, the ecological relevance of autonomy might well be questioned, given the environmental impact of batteries. And, are every-man-for-himself options preferable to a solidarity of exchanges?

Following this type of reasoning, some territories, or some households, claim to use "positive energy". The confusion between energy and electricity is quite common: if an area is able to produce more electricity than it consumes, it does not mean that they are on positive energy since electricity accounts for less than a quarter of the energy consumed. And besides, the intermittence and storage issues come up again: unless the available geographical conditions are favourable, allowing for controllable renewable energy production through solutions such as hydro-electricity or wood power stations, exchanges of electricity are necessary to ensure the availability of electric power at all times. These territories or homes can produce more in average than they consume thanks to wind turbines or solar panels, but they sometimes absorb the electricity produced somewhere else. In one of their report, RTE gives the example of a town which would manage to produce as much electricity as it consumes thanks to wind and photovoltaic devices. But although

> the renewable power installed is around three times the power consumed in peak hours, this town will still need the same network capacity to ensure its supply, except with a substitutive local storage solution for the equivalent amount, a local spare production solution or the organization of selective power shutdowns.
>
> **[RTE]**

For example, the Canary island of El Hierro is presented as energy autonomous thanks to renewable energies. There again, electricity is mixed up with energy, as very few airplanes, boats or cars run on electricity etc. This island with a low population density is lucky to benefit from a very favourable geography – a lot of wind for wind turbines and, above all, a relief offering the possibility of STEP storage, thanks to two huge 150,000-m³ reservoirs separated by a 650-m declivity. The system was inaugurated in 2014 but still needed fuel-oil in 2018 for 44% of the production.

It is a feat of strength nonetheless, and efficiency is likely to improve in the future. But this technology cannot be generalized in higher-population-density and less windy areas, particularly if they do not have hills or mountains to create huge water reservoirs.

2.3   PRIMARY OR FINAL ENERGY?

Should we focus on primary or final energy? The debate is raging because of the impact this has on the choice between the various types of home heating systems. The energy used to keep homes warm is currently recorded as primary energy. By convention, in France when a domestic heating system uses gas or fuel-oil, production or transmission losses, though existing, are not accounted for and primary energy is considered as equal to the final energy spent. On the other hand, when a domestic heating system uses electricity, the European convention stipulates that the amount of the final energy spent is to be multiplied by 2.58 to obtain the corresponding amount of primary energy. Thanks to this coefficient, losses due to the transmission of electricity (around 5%) can be taken into account, and the important losses in power stations in particular. Indeed, when electricity is produced using coal, gas, oil, wood or uranium, most of the primary energy turned into heat is dissipated into the environment without being transformed into electricity. It is thus preferable to load the domestic boiler with coal, gas, fuel-oil or wood rather than to produce electricity meant to supply domestic heating. The 2.58 conventional coefficient is thus perfectly justified when these energy sources are used to produce electricity, which was the case in France when the convention was established. But the reasoning does not make much sense when electricity is produced with uranium, and all the less so with hydroelectric dams, wind turbines or solar panels. In the case of nuclear, the poor yield of power stations and their discharge of a lot of heat cannot be denied. But, is it a serious matter? As we shall see later on, nuclear is not exempt from faults.

It produces waste but very little CO_2 or other air pollutants which makes "nuclear" domestic heating less polluting than the other modes of heating. By the way, the calculation of the primary energy contained in a certain amount of uranium is not easy and derives from a convention, to start with, since the heat released depends on the type of reactor. The 2.58 coefficient is even more questionable when referring to electricity increasingly supplied by wind turbines and photovoltaic panels. We are neither interested in the mechanical energy of the wind driving the turbine blades nor in the solar energy reaching a panel. As with hydroelectricity, by convention, only the electricity put out by these processes is accounted for as primary energy, and not the energy put in. Their yield, though far from perfect, is consequently not taken into account. I consider this calculation method as logical since, the energy source being abundant and non-polluting, a better yield would obviously be preferable but does not constitute an essential criterion. Therefore, applying the same reasoning to nuclear energy would not be illogical. Its yield would not be accounted for because a tiny amount of uranium, which has little impact on the environment, is enough to produce a huge amount of electricity.

The problem is that this famous 2.58 coefficient favours gas domestic heating which, in France, is responsible for more pollution than electric heating. Indeed, the 2012 thermal regulations demanded that the annual consumption of a home in primary energy be less than 50 kWh per m^2. When a home is heated using gas or fuel-oil, the coefficient is 1, but if the heating system is electric, it has to consume less than $50/2.58 = 19.4$ kWh/m^2 per year. As complying with this standard requires a level of insulation that is difficult to achieve, more than 70% of the homes built in France since 2012 are heated by gas. The energy-efficiency diagnosis gives a home heated by electricity a "C" class label, while the same home heated by gas is ranked "A", although it releases more CO_2. Likewise, the energy efficiency diagnosis of an old house will be better if its electric heating is replaced by gas central heating, with more harmful emissions.

The battle is raging between electricity and gas companies to cancel, modify or maintain the 2.58 coefficient or even just account for the final energy of a home. Financial stakes are high. For the time being, the gas lobby has won, to the detriment of polluting emissions and of geopolitical tensions likely to develop in the future concerning our supply of gas. Since the year 2020, regulations have been evolving, but one has to note that for many years, the nuclear lobby has not been the winner.

3 The Importance of Energy

3.1 IMPACTS OF ENERGY ON SOCIETY

We are not aware of the huge amounts of energy we absorb every day. It only feels natural, the same as we feel it natural to use a 100-hp car that has the power of 100 good old horses.

Three miracles of nature – coal, gas and crude oil – account for over 80% of the energy Earthlings currently consume. Since the origin of planet Earth, life was made possible thanks to solar energy, particularly for plants which transform it into organic matter through photosynthesis. Plants partly changed into coal, gas or oil through a million-year-long process. Around 200 years ago, which is just yesterday on the scale of the planet, human beings started to understand the huge power they could draw from the enormous energy godsend made available by nature. The consequences have been considerable. In richer countries, the organization of society was completely modified with farm workers turned into factory workers and then into office workers.

The abundance of energy has largely contributed to the transformation, since the early 19th century, of an agricultural society into the one we live in, in richer countries. This abundance has facilitated the production of food by allowing for the creation of tools, farming machines, irrigation, food preservation, cooking equipment and use of fertilizers. For example, guano, a natural fertilizer, was largely exported from South America to the United States and Europe in the 19th century, thanks to steamships using coal [Mouhot]. In the 20th century, we started producing chemical fertilizers using coal, gas or petroleum. The growing availability of energy has made it easier to access and clean up drinkable water thanks to pumping devices. Energy has improved housing thanks to the fabrication of construction materials, the use of civil engineering vehicles, and heating solutions. It has made transport easier and resulted in a better distribution of ores, materials and food. The abundance of energy has saved time for human beings to devote themselves more to education, health, culture and leisure.

Few people work in fields and factories despite the profusion of available food and goods. The abundance of energy has largely made it possible to replace human beings by machines, therefore granting this society of people the opportunity to take the time to think, to work no more than 35 hours per week, to enjoy paid holidays, comfort and access to culture, healthcare and leisure. The importance of energy is probably largely underestimated in the scope of the incredible evolution over the last 200 years. Without machines or transport systems consuming a lot of energy, most of us would still be working in the fields. These metamorphoses of our societies have made jobs less harassing and, thanks to the manufacturing of machines and materials, part of the labour force has gradually been released to be then employed to increase and transmit knowledge, provide healthcare, assist, inform, manage, etc. This development has contributed to the increase of our life expectancy from 35 years at the beginning of the 19th century to over 80 in today's richer countries. Medicine and the evolution of hygiene have obviously greatly contributed to increasing life expectancy, but it would be impossible to pay people to prevent and cure diseases, to train these people, to keep improving medical techniques, to build hospitals, if all this labour force was required to produce food. And besides, hygiene, building and running hospitals and producing and transporting care equipment require energy.

Today, nearly all French households have running water and a washing machine – more precisely 96%. This domestic appliance has changed family life in comparison with the time when people used to do the washing by hand after drawing water from the nearest well, heating it on the stove, getting some coal or even cutting some wood. Washing machines have become so common that we tend to forget about their importance. Yet, these appliances would not be so common without abundant energy to supply them but also to have them manufactured by supplying a network of energy-greedy factories and the mining equipment to extract, transport and transform ores into steel, glass, motors, electronic components, etc.

The graph in Figure 3.1 shows the percentage of agricultural jobs according to the consumption of energy per inhabitant, each dot representing a country in the world. On the whole, the general trend clearly indicates that this percentage falls when

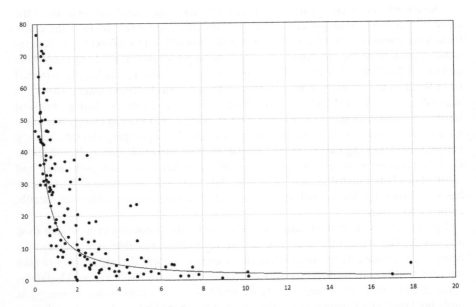

FIGURE 3.1 Percentage of jobs in agriculture according to energy consumption per head in tons of oil equivalent. Each dot represents a country in the world – average values from 2011 to 2015. (Data: World Bank.)

energy consumption increases. It is difficult to have a developed society without consuming a lot of energy. One can obviously be a farmer and happy, but if the population is monopolized by the production of food, it cannot be available for other tasks.

Figure 3.2 shows the graph of life expectancy according to the consumption of energy in some countries. Some of them, Qatar for example, reveal high energy consumption, yet not a very high life expectancy, but apart from this exception, we can observe that people live longer in places where a lot of energy is consumed. Improved life expectancy over time is also due to the decrease of infant mortality for which we can greatly thank growing access to energy.

The human development index (HDI) was created by the United Nations' Development Programme (UNDP) in 1990 with the aim to assess the level of human development in all countries over the world. Life expectancy, educational level and revenue per capita are taken into account. This index appears in Figure 3.3, according to the consumption of energy per person, and the curve clearly reveals that this index is low in places where people consume little energy.

The human capital index was created by the World Bank in 2018. It measures the human capital that a child born today is likely to reach when aged 18. It incorporates the child's survival expectancy at the age of 18, their health condition, the duration of their schooling and the knowledge acquired. In Figure 3.4, this index has been drawn according to the amount of energy consumed per individual in each country. Here again, we can observe the difficulties faced by countries with little access to energy.

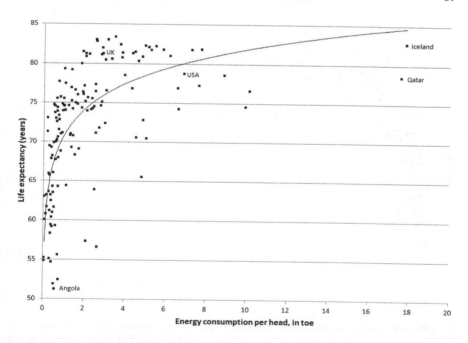

FIGURE 3.2 Life expectancy according to energy consumption per head in toe. Each dot represents a country in the world. Average values from 2011 to 2015. (Data: World Bank.)

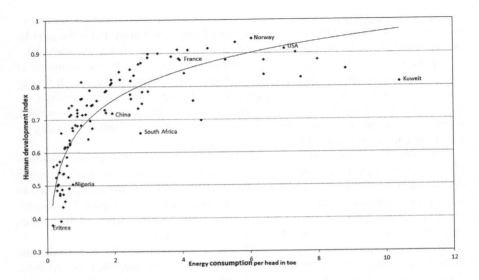

FIGURE 3.3 Human development index according to energy consumption per head in toe. Each dot represents a country in the world. Average values from 2009 to 2012. (Data: World Bank.)

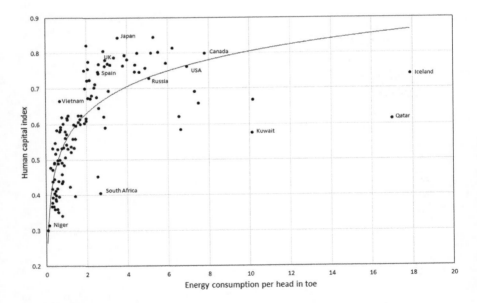

FIGURE 3.4 Human capital index according to energy consumption per head in toe. Each dot represents a country in the world. Average consumption from 2011 to 2015. (Data: World Bank.)

Energy helps satisfy vital needs, and many poor countries need more energy to improve their people's living conditions.

These curves reveal a "saturation" effect: your life will not be twice as long if you consume twice as much energy. As a matter of fact, some countries waste energy, and dividing the consumption of energy by two would not imply the division of life expectancy by two. There must be room for improvement in some richer countries which should manage to consume less without any serious consequences. But it seems to be difficult to live in a developed country with less than 3 toe (or 3,000 koe) per capita and per year (France was at about 3.8 toe in 2018). If the 7.5 billion human beings on the planet had equal access to these 3 toe, which would imply a large reduction of the richer countries' consumption (5.5 toe per capita in Australia, 6.9 in the USA, 7.7 in Canada, 17.8 in Iceland), the amount of energy available in the world per year would reach 22,500 million toe while world consumption in 2018 was 13,684 million of toe [BP]. With 10 billion individuals on the planet in 2050, the amount of energy made available to Earthlings would have to be doubled.

3.2   ENERGY AND GROWTH

Economic activity, i.e. all the actions that the human population has to carry out to meet their needs thanks to the production of goods and services, requires energy to mine raw materials, to transform, transport and sell them, to manage the related administrations, provide services etc.

Gross domestic product (GDP) reflects the economic activity, i.e. human beings' activity. This index is questionable as it does not necessarily reflect human happiness. It may increase following a natural disaster if reconstruction requires activity. Moreover, some useful non-mercantile activities are not included in its calculation while they consume energy all the same. However, GDP is probably the most revealing index of human activity. A vast majority of policy makers look at its increase, as the GDP per capita gives an approximate measure of the living standard through people's access to goods and services.

Figure 3.5 shows the evolution of the world's GDP in the last 2,000 years, as reconstituted by some university lecturers. It makes it clear that GDP stagnated until the industrial revolution at the beginning of the 19th century, when coal started to be exploited.

In richer countries, GDP has considerably increased since the Second World War, at the same time as the consumption of crude oil. Figure 3.6 shows the evolution of the world's energy consumption from 1800 to 2015. Up to the end of the 19th century, people would consume wood. Coal became dominant during the first half of the 20th century, and crude oil in the second half. We observe a strong growth from the Second World War on. The arrival of petroleum and gas did not reduce the consumption of coal. The arrival of hydro-electricity, nuclear power and renewables, which hardly appear on the figure, did not induce a decrease in the consumption of fossil energies.

Figure 3.7 shows the evolution of GDP and of energy consumption between 1965 and 2018: their growth is evidence of the increase of human activities.

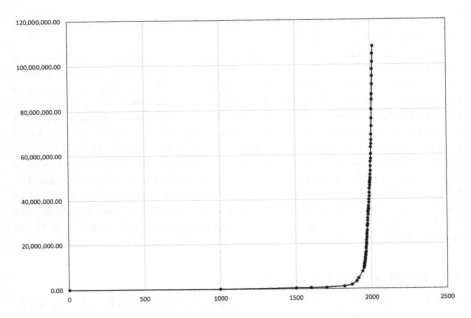

FIGURE 3.5 World GDP, in million dollars from year 0, adjusted for inflation and expressed in international-$ in 2011 prices. (Source: Our World in Data.)

The growth of GDP has always been linked to growing energy consumption. Indeed, as we can see in Figure 3.7, today's world energy consumption grows less rapidly than GDP – energy intensity is decreasing, as we say – but, up to now, economic growth has never been durably combined with a fall in energy consumption.

In Figure 3.8, the data are the same as above but the energy curve is drawn according to world GDP, each dot representing a year. The correlation appears clearly. The ideal situation would be that energy consumption would decrease while GDP increases, i.e. that this curve would durably drop. But there is no sign of such a trend starting.

The curves in Figure 3.9 show the evolution of annual variation percentages of the world's GDP from 1965 to 2018. The correlation between the two elements is obvious. According to Jean-Marc Jancovici, who drew this sort of graph a long time before I did, the variations in energy consumption often precede those of GDP [Jancovici Web].

According to the economists G. Giraud and Z. Kahraman [Giraud Kahraman], a 60% rise of the world's GDP requires a 100% rise in energy consumption – i.e. a multiplication by two – which otherwise means that a 3% annual rise of the world's GDP implies a 5% rise of energy consumption. According to them, the role of energy would largely be underestimated.

Thierry Carminel, an engineer and author of several books dealing with the links between economy and energy, asserts – in "L'impossible découplage entre énergie et croissance" [Carminel] – that "it is easy to demonstrate that the growth rate of GDP

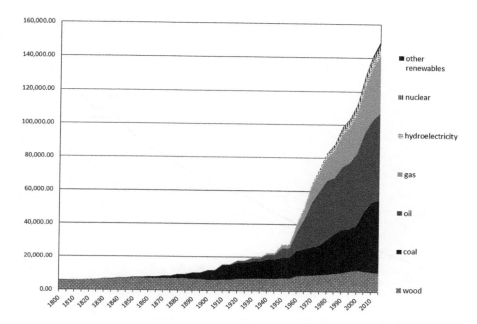

FIGURE 3.6 World energy per source from 1800 to 2015 in TWh. (Source: https://ourworl dindata.org/grapher/global-primary-energy, Vaclav Smil (2017). Energy Transitions: Global and National Perspectives. BP Statistical Review of World Energy [data concerning fossil energies seem to be expressed in terms of primary energy, and the others in terms of final energy].)

per capita roughly equals the sum of the rise in energy consumption per capita plus the evolution of the GDP's energy intensity" and that the latter only improves very slowly.

According to Tim Morgan, the economy is not a matter of money but a function of excess energy, in other words of the energy available to us.

According to the economist Maarten Van Mourik, specializing in the analysis of the petroleum market, and to Oskar Slingerland, a petroleum industry executive, "energy-supply problems will inevitably restrict the global growth in GDP". "Economic growth and real wealth are created by work – which relies on machines and energy – and not by moving loads of money and virtual debts" [Mourik].

Since the 1960s, petroleum has been the world's prime source of energy. In 1973, while the demand in crude oil had continuously been increasing and the price of the barrel was stable, oil-producing countries agreed on a petroleum embargo against several western countries who supported Israel in the Yom Kippur War. Consequently, the barrel price was multiplied by three between 1972 and 1975, and it was the first oil crisis. In 1979, the revolution in Iran triggered the second crisis. Both these price rises perfectly appear in Figure 3.10, which shows the evolution of the barrel price from 1945 to 2010. These oil shortages sapped economic growth, provoked economic crises, unemployment, public deficits etc. What is also clearly visible is that the record barrel price was reached in 2008, just before what was

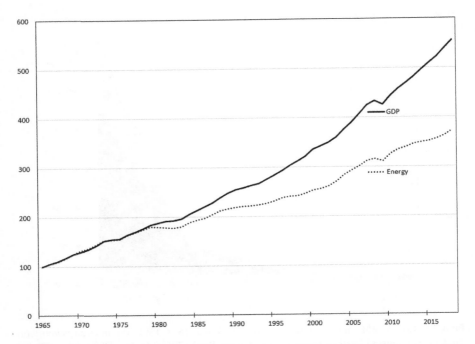

FIGURE 3.7 Evolution of world GDP in 2010 constant dollars and of primary energy consumed around the world –100 base in 1965. (Source: World Bank/*BP statistical review of world energy 2019* [BP].)

dubbed the "financial crisis". The 2008 peak price did not result from a conflict or an embargo, but probably just from the supply-and-demand relationship, as demand had become higher than production capacities. According to some people, the 2008 crisis is largely linked to the oil shortage which could no longer fuel the economy. CNRS economist Gaël Giraud asserted in 2014 [Giraud interview] that

> our economies have taken on debt to compensate for the oil price rise! With very cheap credit at the time, the oil-crisis was made relatively painless. At the same time, monetary policy, deregulation and the short-sightedness of the banking system also provoked the inflation of the subprime bubble, the bursting of which, in 2007, triggered the crisis. Therefore, the remedy which helped smooth the oil crisis also provoked the worst financial crisis in history, which was in turn largely responsible for the current public debt crisis, the weakening of the Euro, etc. It is as if we were now paying for the cost of the third oil-crisis.

In fact, the deep cause of this crisis was not only financial but also physical. Tim Jackson, a British economist, specializing in sustainable development, wrote in 2009 [Jackson]:

> It now seems likely that the very high prices reached by the main raw materials in mid-2008 partly resulted from speculation and, for the rest, of identifiable supply issues such as the limitation of refining capacities in case of high demand.

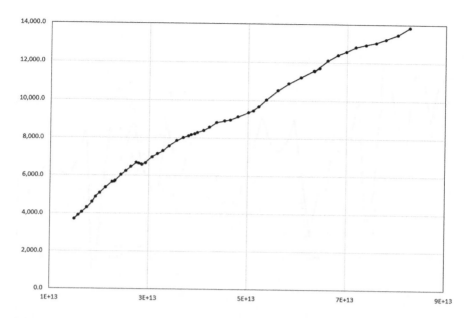

FIGURE 3.8 Energy consumed around the world in millions of toe, according to world GDP in 2010 constant US dollars. (Source: World Bank/*BP statistical review of world energy 2019* [BP].)

In his book – *Oil, Power and War: A Dark History* – Mathieu Auzanneau, a specialist in oil-related questions, suggests the following analysis: "the increase in the barrel rate strongly fuelled inflation, which, in reaction, triggered a rise in interest rates, which provoked the bursting of the subprime bubble" [Auzanneau]. In their book entitled *The Misunderstood Crisis*, Maarten Van Mourik, and Oskar Slingerland wrote: "the development of the financial bubble that the world experienced until 2007 was only due to the abundance of cheap oil"; "we know why the price of crude oil went up: because of the agony of a system based on the abundance of an energy source on which we have drawn lavishly"; "there is a characteristic in the 2008 crisis … that makes it different from any other previous crisis … as the actual demand met with the limits of supply" [Mourik].

The lack of energy most probably played an important role in the so-called 2008 financial crisis. The slight drop in energy consumption in France since this crisis has most probably been linked to the stagnation, if not the unprecedented fall of France's GDP and of the French people's purchasing power since 2007, which, according to economist François Bourguignon's article in the March 16th, 2019 copy of the newspaper "Le Monde", explained the French "*gilets jaunes*" crisis, a social movement that started in autumn 2018.

Figure 3.11 shows the evolution of oil consumption in the United States from 1965 to 2015, which is similar to that of rich countries. We observe that it went through a peak in 2005 and started to fall from 2006 on, before the beginning of the crisis, which corroborates the idea that the shortage in oil generated the crisis. The world

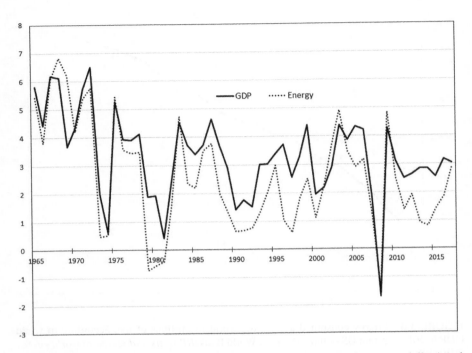

FIGURE 3.9 Evolution of world GDP annual variation percentages (in current dollars) and of primary energy consumption. (Data: World Bank/*BP statistical review of world energy 2019* [BP].)

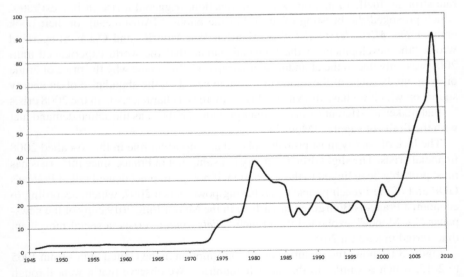

FIGURE 3.10 Evolution of the oil barrel price in New York in current US dollars. (Source: International Energy Agency.)

FIGURE 3.11 Evolution of oil consumption in the USA from 1965 to 2016, in millions of toe. (Source: *BP statistical review of world energy 2017.*)

production of oil stabilized from 2004 to 2008, as shown by Figure 3.12. The economic crisis obviously provoked a consecutive fall of demand which, combined with the arrival of non-conventional oils on the market, led to considerably lower prices in the following years. For how many years?

When there is a growth of the GDP – i.e. so-called "growth" in short – it means that activity increases. Firms recruit more, and unemployment tends to decrease. They make more profit, part of which can be passed on to the wage-earners whose purchasing power increases. Social contributions increase, pension and healthcare funds are thus better funded, the state collects more tax revenues and can lower taxes or invest in public services, social benefits, education, research, culture etc. This intensification of the exchanges of goods and services is logically meant to increase people's comfort. If wealth is measured according to the amount of goods and services made available, economic growth allows for a larger amount of wealth, hence allowing some to get richer without taking from others. Sharing a cake that is getting bigger makes things easier for the ruling authorities.

In most countries, the state spends more than the revenue it gets, and it borrows money regularly.

If the interest rate of the debt is higher than the GDP growth rate, a snowball effect may make the debt grow automatically. If, on the contrary, the interest rate is lower than the growth rate, the weight of the debt decreases.

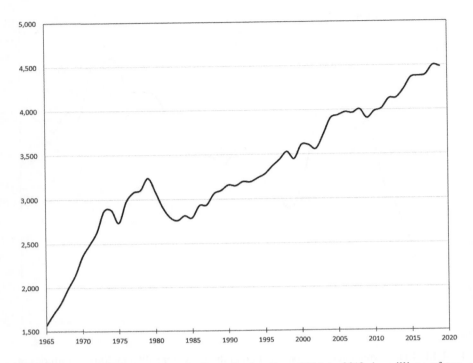

FIGURE 3.12 Evolution of world oil production from 1964 to 2019, in millions of toe. (Source: *BP statistical review of world energy 2020.*)

"The only thing that might automatically increase the State's and the Social Security's revenues is growth" [Musolino].

It is thus easy to understand why policymakers look for economic growth.

The environmental awareness of recent years is an incentive to consume less energy, not to waste so much, not to throw away so much. Indeed the finite nature of energy resources and the numerous drawbacks related to energy consumption must incite us to do so. But this implies lowering production, to sell less, to have fewer activities, hence provoking fundamental questions: is economic growth compatible with a reduction of energy and resource consumption? Is perpetual economic growth possible? Can we keep consuming more and more energy, surface areas, rare metals, various ores, water?

According to some economists, the problem is *nothing but* technical [Musolino]. They believe future technologies and green growth will produce miracles. According to sustainable development optimists, new technologies, and particularly the ones related to information technology, will manage to disconnect economy from energy. In my opinion, technique can only obey the laws of physics which have their own limits. These technologies are operational in rich countries only because the products we need are manufactured by energy-hungry industries in Asia. Besides, the development of digital technologies has implied the rise of enormous and very energy-hungry data centres. Digital technology already absorbs 10% of the world's

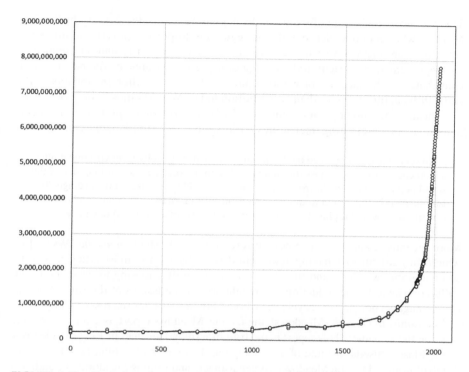

FIGURE 3.13 Evolution of the world population for 2,000 years. (Source: Our World in Data.)

electricity. If we take everything into account, a smartphone would consume as much energy as a refrigerator. According to the think tank *The Shift Project*, the digital sector was responsible, in 2019, for 4% the world's greenhouse gas emissions, i.e. more than civil air transport, and its consumption will increase by 9% per year. Of course, some economic sectors have a lower impact than others, but I am not convinced that growth might be green.

Since time immemorial the world's population has been growing. Figure 3.13 shows that it increased slowly for many centuries. Its growth started to speed up shortly after the end of the Middle Ages and soared in the 19th century with the industrial revolution and the consumption of fossil energies.

The question of economic growth is partly related to demographic growth, the latter generating the former. There are two conflicting positions:

- Encouraging demographic growth, which fuels economic growth and increases the amount of wealth in order to fight against poverty.
- Considering that perpetual economic growth is not possible since it requires an increasingly higher consumption of natural resources, energy in particular. Considering that sharing resources between larger numbers of people mathematically generates a decrease in wealth per capita.

This second vision was put forward at the beginning of the 19th century by Thomas Malthus who recommended population regulation to prevent poverty. Malthus has actually been disproved so far: a massive use of fossil energy and, consequently, the improvement of agricultural techniques, hygiene measures, medicine, etc., have contributed to the increase of world population from one billion inhabitants in the early 19th century to more than seven billion today. Was Malthus wrong, or was he just ahead of his time by a few centuries? In *Moins nombreux, plus heureux*, a collaborative book presenting interesting considerations [Sourrouille], one can read that

> all the ecologists that worked on the question of the demography-to-environment interaction end up to more or less the same conclusion: if we expect a vast majority of the world population to benefit from a life style comparable to the one of the average 2010 European, this population would be around one billion, on the additional condition that this life style would rapidly become thriftier in the use of energy and raw materials.

More recently, Canadian and Swedish researchers published an article [Wynes] in which they affirm that having fewer children is by far the most efficient way to combat global warming and that "an American family choosing to have one fewer child contribute to the reduction of greenhouse gas emissions at the same level as 684 teenagers choosing to recycle the whole of their waste for the rest of their lives".

The Limits to Growth [Meadows], the famous Meadows report, is a very important work on these themes. This report is the fruit of a study launched in 1972 by scientists of the Massachusetts Institute of Technology at the request of a think tank known as "Club of Rome". Donella Meadows, Jorgen Randers and Dennis Meadows, the authors, tried to model the world by computer with action and retroaction loops, such as "If more agricultural inputs, then more food", "If more food, then more population", "If more population, then more energy consumption, more pollution or more resource depletion".

In 2004, these authors reviewed their work and observed that their 1972 projections were on the right track and tried again to forecast the consequences of exponential growth in a finite world. Their conclusions are frightening: to sum up, a collapse of society will be avoided if, very quickly, the world population and industrial production are stabilized, the efficiency of the use of resources is improved, pollution is limited, etc. Most scenarios lead to a collapse of our civilization, i.e. to a sharp drop in life expectancy and in population as a consequence, in industrial production, in food and services per capita and in the human well-being index. The authors of this report have been largely criticized. Yet, many civilizations have collapsed throughout history, as explained by Jared Diamond in *Collapse: How Societies Choose to Fail or Survive* [Diamond]. The civilizations of Easter Island's inhabitants, of the Anasazi tribes in the South-West of the United States, of the Maya people in central America, etc., collapsed mainly because of environmental reasons.

3.3 THE KAYA IDENTITY

In order to limit global warming, human beings must reduce their greenhouse gas emissions, mainly CO_2 resulting from the use of fossil energy. The identity introduced in 1993, by the Japanese economist Yoichi Kaya, helps us to simply become aware of the challenge represented by the task in question.

$$CO_2 = \text{Population} \times \frac{PIB}{\text{Population}} \times \frac{\text{Energy}}{PIB} \times \frac{CO_2}{\text{Energy}}$$

From a purely mathematical point of view, it is easy to observe that simplifications can be made and that this equation is correct. If CO_2 emissions are to be reduced, the product of the four terms must decrease. On a global scale, the experts from the Intergovernmental Panel on Climate Change (IPCC) consider that CO_2 emissions have to be reduced by 45% by 2030 as compared to 2010, and by at least 91% by 2050 [IPCC 2018] to succeed in limiting global warming.

The first term concerns the population. There were 6.9 billion individuals on Earth in 2010 and, according to the UN, the world population should reach 9.8 billion by 2050, i.e. a multiplication by 1.42.

The second term, GDP/Population, reflects the amount of wealth per capita. What the vast majority of human beings wish is to increase the amount of goods and services available to them. Decreasing this term implies decreasing the purchasing power. From 2010 to 2018, it rose by 1.61% per year, and many people would like it to improve further. At this pace, it will be multiplied by 1.9 (+90%) by 2050 as compared to 2010.

The third term, Energy/GDP, represents the energy intensity of the GDP. We have seen how energy and GDP are related to each other. Energy efficiency, through which we can have an effect on this term by consuming less for an eventually equivalent service, is crucial. Fortunately, energy intensity improves and this term decreases. From 2010 to 2018, it went down by 1.26% per year. At this pace, it will be multiplied by 0.6 by 2050.

The fourth term, CO_2/Energy, reflects the amount of greenhouse gas in energy. It can decrease if fossil energies are replaced by energies emitting no greenhouse gases, whether renewable or nuclear, or, more simply, if coal power stations are replaced by gas power stations, which are less polluting. This may be what allowed a small drop of 0.45% per year from 2010 to 2018. At this pace, this term will be multiplied by 0.84 by 2050.

Let us now multiply the four 2050 projections: $1.42 \times 1.9 \times 0.6 \times 0.84 = 1.36$. But we should get a product under 0.1 to limit global warming to 1.5°. The trend is clearly not the right one! To reach this objective by 2050 without changing the first two terms, each of the last ones should be under 0.2, which means that energy intensity as well as the greenhouse gas content should be improved by three to four times. What a considerable challenge!

3.4 ENERGY AND EMPLOYMENT

The energy-hungry machines appeared and replaced human beings, allowing for productivity gains. Thanks to energy, production requires less labour. Energy-hungry machines have allowed for the production of larger amounts of commodities and for the labour force to be moved from fields to factories, then from factories to offices, and then to unemployment. It is just pure logic: energy is highly valuable to us because it reduces our workload.

Energy consumption has largely contributed to alleviate poverty by improving living conditions, but it has paradoxically jacked up unemployment. Unemployed people do not live in luxury but, fortunately, most jobless in rich countries live in a decent home, can eat every day, have access to medical care, can send their children to school etc. Nineteenth-century workers' living conditions were not any better than today's jobless. The unemployment issue is often seen as the major problem in our rich societies. It is definitely a problem, but poverty is even worse, and we must be careful not to curb unemployment while increasing poverty. Unemployment would perhaps decrease without the energy used for agricultural and civil engineering machines as all the work would have to be done manually, but I am not sure poverty would actually decline. Housing access would be more complex, so would access to food probably. Energy makes it possible to make machines work instead of men, hence requiring less labour force. Energy thus makes life easier, but, without growth, it decreases employment.

I wonder about what I hear, when people say that such and such energy is good because it creates jobs. If we push this reasoning to extremes, we would be able to create jobs by having human beings pedal. The simple calculations above show how ridiculously low this production of energy would be as compared to the time spent. The interest of energy is actually to have less work to do! It is precisely with the aim of having less to do that, for centuries, human beings have used the energy of oxen to draw ploughs, of the wind to push boats, of river streams to grind corn etc. Creating work is not a typical quality for energy. To tackle the unemployment issue, it would surely be better to look at the ways to share wealth and employment rather than to rely on green growth.

3.5   DEGROWTH

As perpetual growth is not likely to be possible, degrowth is advocated by some people nowadays.

Jean Gadrey, a French economist, defines himself as a growth objector. In his book *Adieu la Croissance* [Gadrey], he clearly explains that perpetual growth is impossible and suggests interesting clues to live without it. For example, he explains that creating jobs in the field of housing insulation or with the switching from conventional to organic agriculture is possible. It is certainly true and desirable, but with access to food and housing becoming more complicated, we may fear that these fundamental needs would be less easily met in the future.

In the same state of mind is Tim Jackson, a sustainable development specialist wrote *Prosperity Without Growth: Economics for a Finite Planet* [Jackson]. He explains that economic growth has never been disconnected from physically induced fluxes, that there is no prospect for this disconnection to occur in the near future, that "**even the scale of the required disconnection … challenges the imagination**", that this disconnection is a myth. He explains that an economy based on the sale of non-material services – sport-clubs, repair and maintenance services, artistic activities, goods renting etc. – cannot generate economic production with permanent growth and that "when the impacts these activities are responsible for are fully taken into account, many of them are revealed as resource-greedy as the manufacturing sectors". He suggests, quite rightly, investing in energy efficiency, recycling solutions, low-carbon technologies, waste reduction, reforestation etc. but he specifies that **there is "no existing coherent sustainable development-oriented macroeconomic framework"**. This book provides food for thought, but, as opposed to the previous one, it does not suggest any pattern clearly showing the way to run a degrowth-based society. I was actually left unsatisfied, and I still do not know how a leader should fund public services, healthcare and retirement pensions in that particular world. To my knowledge, there is no existing economic model to manage a degrowth-based society.

A previous French prime minister, Michel Rocard, declared in the newspaper *La Tribune* in 2015:

> We are experiencing a situation that is extremely aggravating inequalities. Poverty is decreasing in our world thanks to the emergence of many countries but it is slightly increasing in France on average, and even flaring up, according to some. My intuition is that degrowth would firstly intensify these inequalities and would lead us straight to something like a civil war. I do not understand how some clever people with an environmentally friendly sensitivity are not taking this into account. Either you suffer degrowth and it is a catastrophe, or you provoke it and it is even worse. This option must thus be ruled out, for public order reasons.

My impression is that the people who do not fear degrowth are often considering that today's world is not good, that it used to be better in the old days, that technology and energy consumption have mainly created problems, pollution, diseases and is responsible for the destruction of our planet. It is less fearful to hope for a return to the past if you think that the good old days were definitely best. This is not my opinion: scientific knowledge, technology, progress obviously have their drawbacks. Innovations require our society to be reconsidered and adapted. But I think that energy-hungry technologies have so far largely contributed to improving human well-being, and I am afraid that degrowth might not be a heartening project, even if it is likely to be inevitable.

4 Pollution, Risks and Problems Related to Energy Sources

All energy sources have their drawbacks. Clean energy does not exist. Indeed, any human construction impacts our environment, uses space and natural resources and contributes to various types of pollution.

4.1 GLOBAL WARMING

Everyone has surely heard, by now, of global warming. This phenomenon is undeniable. Just go hiking in the mountains and compare the current situation of glaciers to what we can see in some old photographs and you will observe a dramatic retreat. As a matter of fact, this does not prove that this warming is of human origin, created or amplified by greenhouse gas emissions related to human activities, and particularly by the amount of CO_2 released by burning coal, petroleum or gas.

The overwhelming majority of scientists dealing with these matters consider that human activities are largely responsible for global warming. CO_2 increases the greenhouse effect, which hinders the Earth's infrared radiation and the diffusion of heat towards space. The solar energy reaching the Earth is thus increasingly trapped because of CO_2.

Fossil energies come from plants which have slowly stored the carbon present in the atmosphere for millions of years through the effect of solar energy and photosynthesis. At the beginning of the 19th century, human beings started burning coal, gas and petroleum, thus releasing into the atmosphere, in around 200 years, half the amount of carbon it had taken millions of years to store. Two hundred years, compared to millions of years, just means "all at once", and thinking that it might have consequences does not seem stupid at all to me.

For a long time, emissions due to deforestation were dominant among all CO_2 emissions: when burning, trees release the carbon they have stored while growing. Since the mid-20th century, emissions due to coal, petroleum and gas became much higher than those due to deforestation. Today, they easily account for ten times as much.

The potential consequences of global warming are huge and not very cheering: falling agricultural outputs, decreasing water resources in most dry regions, decreasing flow of water springs fed by melting ice and snow, increase in extreme meteorological phenomena – torrential rains, storms and drought – increase in forest fires, extension of areas infested by diseases such as cholera or malaria, higher flooding risks, rising sea level, etc.

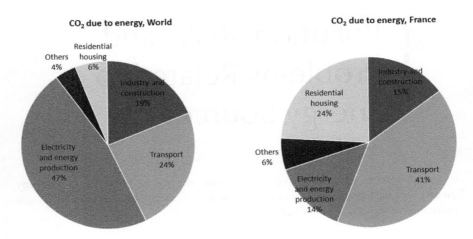

CO₂ due to energy, World   CO₂ due to energy, France

FIGURE 4.1 CO_2 emissions due to energy per sector. (Sources: AIE 2017 [2015 figures]/ European Environment Agency 2018/Commissariat général au développement durable [Datalab climat]).

CO_2 is not the only greenhouse gas. Methane, which is mainly produced by agriculture, nitrous oxide from agriculture and industries, and other gases also contribute to global warming. All emissions are generally accounted for in "CO_2 equivalent". At the world level, about 85% of greenhouse gas emissions come from the energy sector. At the French level, the percentage is only 70% [Datalab climat], probably thanks to lower emissions from the production of electricity. Figure 4.1 shows the origins of CO_2 emissions due to energy production across the world and in France. Across the world, energy production (mainly electricity: 39%) is the primary cause of CO_2 emissions. There is nothing surprising about this since the primary energy source across the world for the production of electricity is coal, i.e. the largest CO_2-emitting source. We must thus come to grips with the problem and replace coal by sources emitting less CO_2 for the production of electricity. In France, since electricity is mainly produced through nuclear or hydraulic energy, which are very low greenhouse-gas-emitting sources, the transport sector is the primary cause of emissions, more than half of which concerns private motor vehicles. What have we done in France for 20 years to fight against global warming? Instead of dealing with transport systems and insulating buildings massively, we have installed wind turbines and photovoltaic panels in order to replace electricity that was already largely decarbonized. In these conditions, it is not surprising that French emissions do not decrease much! In their first report, published in June 2019 [HCC], the *Haut Conseil pour le Climat*, an organization in charge of providing notices and recommendations about the reduction of greenhouse gases in France, wrote: "the real average annual 1.1% reduction of greenhouse gas emissions over the recent period is nearly twice as slow as it should be considering the pace required to achieve the objectives"; "most current measures only concern a marginal reduction of emissions". This report underlined the necessity to deal with transport – petroleum – and heating

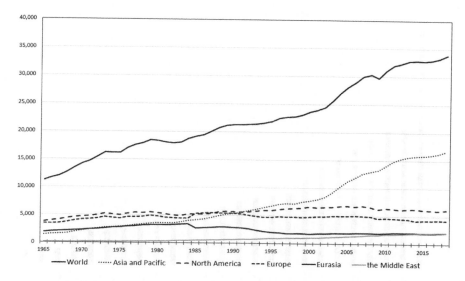

FIGURE 4.2 Evolution of CO_2 emissions (in million tons) from 1965 to 2018. (Source: *BP statistical review of world energy 2019* [BP].)

systems – mainly gas. According to the figures provided by this authority, the first thing to do to curb emissions over the French territory is to fight against motor cars, which is less popular than promoting the installation of photovoltaic panels which are a source of profit for their owners.

Figure 4.2 shows the world evolution of CO_2 emissions and of the major greenhouse-gas-emitting areas: Asia and the Pacific, North America, Europe and Eurasia, the Middle-East. We observe that world emissions are increasing. There was a slight drop with the 2008 crisis, but it was followed by a new significant increase. Now, according to the IPCC, if the 1.5°C rise in temperatures were to be maintained, we would need to decrease greenhouse gas emissions by 45% by 2030, compared with 2010.

Asian countries are the ones increasing their emissions while North America and Europe are fairly steady, situations that are consistent with these regions' energy consumption. This is not surprising, since one coal power station was opened in China each week from 2005 to 2014. But it would be incongruous to shift the blame onto Asian countries as their emissions are largely due to the manufacturing of the products we buy from them. The *Haut Conseil pour le Climat* – French climate authority – declared in June 2019 that, concerning France's greenhouse gas emissions, emissions related to imported goods accounted for 60% of the national emissions in 2015 [HCC]. In other words, our real greenhouse gas emissions have to be multiplied by 1.6 compared to the national territory's actual emissions.

Moreover, to be fair, it might be necessary to compare emissions per person. This is what Figure 4.3 is about: although China is responsible for over 27% of the world's emissions, these actually account for a far lower amount per person than America's.

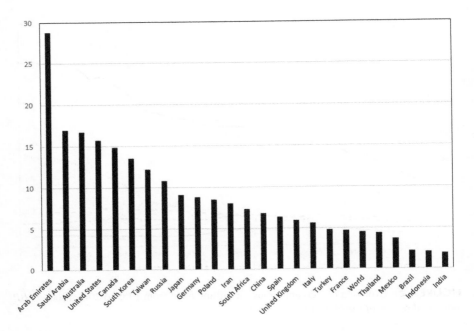

FIGURE 4.3 CO_2 emissions per head in 2018 in countries responsible for more than 0.8% CO_2 emissions in tons of CO_2 per head. (Source: *BP statistical review of world energy 2019/* World Bank.)

The larger pollution-emitters per capita are oil-producing countries. France is not doing so badly, with lower pollution than Germany which is still regularly given as an environmentally friendly example: in 2018, the average German emitted 1.88 times as much CO_2 as the average French citizen.

There is a recurrent debate about the evolution of the CO_2 emissions the Germans are responsible for, as they are sometimes blamed for compensating for their gradual nuclear phase out with very polluting coal power stations. Figure 4.4 shows the evolution of Germany's and France's CO_2 emissions since 1965. We observe that French emissions have dropped with the commissioning of the nuclear power plants from the late 1970s on. We observe that German emissions dropped in the 1990 and 2000 decades, and that they stabilized after 2011 with the shutdown of part of their nuclear pool. Over the last ten years, the drop has been more important in France: –15.7% in France from 2009 to 2019, –9.3% in Germany. German emissions dropped more in 2017, 2018 and 2019, which might be partly due to the numerous wind turbines which allowed for coal power stations to reduce their production. The worse your initial situation is, the easier it is to progress. However, the long-term trend is not that clear, as CO_2 emissions increased in both countries in 2015 and 2016. German renewable energy since 2011 seems to have helped the nuclear production of electricity to drop more than CO_2 emissions, which is a debatable option. In 2019, Germany announced that the use of coal would be abandoned by 2038 and all nuclear power

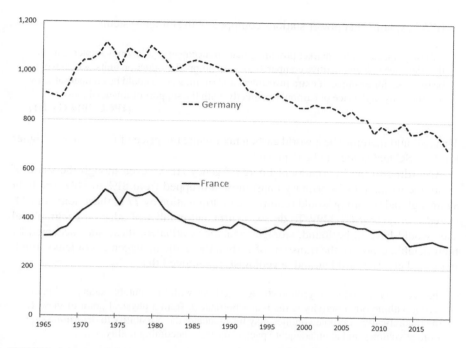

FIGURE 4.4 Evolution of CO_2 emissions in Germany and France from 1965 to 2019. (Source: *BP statistical review of world energy 2020* [BP].)

stations would be shut down by 2022, but we will see that the opposite would have been preferable.

Beware not to gloat too soon about the drop in emissions that can be observed on these two curves. They are largely due to deindustrialisation affecting all rich countries. The carbon footprint, which takes into account indirect emissions due to the manufacturing and transportation of products we import, increased by 54% for France between 1990 and 2012 [Empreinte]. According to the French National Economic Statistics Institute (INSEE) the average French citizen's carbon footprint increased slightly from 2014 to 2017.

One possible solution envisaged to decrease the amount of CO_2 in the atmosphere is to store it underground. This technology is called the capture and storage of carbon (CSC). Carbon from coal power stations, for example, can be captured and injected into deep geological layers. The most common potential sites are saline aquifers (porous rocks), oil and gas depleted fields and unexploited coal seams. Of course, the capture is never complete and, above all, it consumes energy!

In 2019, there were only 18 CSC sites in use worldwide. Moreover, they essentially concern natural gas extraction wells. In these landfills, methane is mixed with CO_2, so the latter has to be separated in these exploitations for the methane to be usable. In these cases, storage is thus a matter of economic necessities but not of an environmental approach.

IPCC explains that power stations equipped with storage systems

> will only appear on the market providing that an incentive regulation is implemented or that they become competitive compared to non-equipped production units, which would be the case, for example, if extra investment and running costs could be compensated by a sufficiently high price of carbon, or, directly, with the support of financial aids.
>
> **[IPCC 2014 GT III]**

There should therefore be a world carbon tax raising the price of fossil energy higher for the CSC technology to be deployed.

According to the International Energy Agency (IEA), even though the share of fossil energy sources in primary consumption dropped from 81% to 60%, the fight against global warming would require the multiplication by 77 of the amount of CO_2 stored each year [SPS 329]! To do so, a sufficient number of adapted geographical sites would have to be found, storage capacities evaluated, these sites accepted by their neighbourhoods, the transport of carbon there, the management of leaks, funding found etc. Bernard Durand, a geologist, maintained that

> the necessity to find underground storage facilities with indisputable safety and interfering with no other activity is the major bottleneck from a physical point of view. If the theoretically available volumes may be adequate, the possibility to determine safe storage volumes and at an adequate pace is far from becoming reality.

Therefore, I find it clear that we cannot rely much on this CSC technology to curb global warming.

4.2   DANGERS OF FOSSIL ENERGY SOURCES AND WOOD

- Natural gas is composed of 95% methane (CH_4). Its combustion emits CO_2 – hence contributing to global warming – and fine dust particles, nitrogen oxides, carbon monoxide, sulphur oxide etc. These substances are obviously harmful to health. Gas may also provoke fire, explosions, asphyxia in case of leaks etc. Methane leaks contribute to global warming, as methane is a powerful greenhouse gas. The exploitation of non-conventional gases – shale gas, for example – is a water-polluting factor and causes many more methane leaks than conventional gases. Natural gas is not the most dangerous of all fossil energy, but it is far from harmless. Yet, its worldwide consumption increased by 34% between 2009 and 2019 (see Figure 4.5).
- Petroleum emits CO_2 when burning, hence contributing to global warming – fine dust particles, nitrogen oxide, carbon monoxide, benzene, sulphur dioxide – responsible for acid rain. It generates oil slicks, tanker degassing at sea, fire, explosions and greenhouse gas leaks when extracted. The exploitation of non-conventional oils – shale oil, bituminous sand – pollutes water and consumes a lot of … oil – around one barrel for three or four extracted. The world crude oil consumption increased by 15% between 2009 and 2019 (see Figure 3.12).

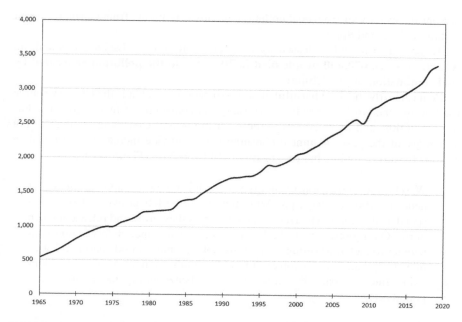

FIGURE 4.5 Evolution of world natural gas consumption from 1965 to 2019, in millions of toe. (Source: *BP statistical review of world energy 2020*.)

- Coal combustion generates CO_2 emissions, greatly contributing to global warming, fine dust particles, sulphur dioxide, carbon monoxide, arsenic (!), fluorine (good for your teeth in small doses but poisonous otherwise), thallium, selenium, lead – very harmful – cadmium, mercury and even radioactivity! Coal extraction processes cause thousands of deaths per year through mining accidents, silicosis and other coal-miner diseases. Coal extraction processes may release methane, which amplifies global warming. In Germany, for the exploitation of open-cast coal mines over a surface area of more than 500 km², 60 villages had to be obliterated and 10,000 people displaced [CEW]. On "Euractiv", the European website, one can read that

> in the European Union, over 18,000 people die every year from the effects of the air pollution caused by the production of coal and coal power stations, according to NGO Health and Environment Alliance (HEAL) quoted in *Atlas du Charbon 2015*.

The "Europe's Dark Cloud" [EDK] report, published in 2016 by WWF, HEAL, Climate Action Network Europe and the Sandbag organization, considers that **European coal power stations are responsible for up to 23,000 early deaths every year!** Epidemiologists' estimates show a strong incidence of fine dust particles, nitrogen oxides and sulphur dioxides in cerebrovascular accidents, heart diseases, cancers, lung diseases etc. French power stations cause 390 deaths every year, British ones 2,860, German ones 4,350 and Polish ones 5,830. In France, 1,380 persons die every year from coal pollution, mainly originating from Germany, Great Britain, Poland and Spain.

According to a study released by the Natural Resources Defense Council, an American NGO, **670,000 people died in 2012 due to the pollution generated by coal combustion in just China!**

Coal is clearly the most harmful of all fossil energies. Yet, it is the primary source used across the world to produce electricity. Its consumption increased a lot during the 2000s, and its reserves are the most important. Coal is unfortunately not an energy of the past. Its annual consumption worldwide increased in 2014, then seemed to start dropping, but rose again in 2017 and 2018 (Figure 4.6).

- Wood is the world's fourth energy source. It is renewable and has an almost neutral carbon balance, providing that it can be left growing at the same speed as it is cut down. Trees store carbon as they grow and release it when burnt. On a global scale, the balance is negative, since deforestation contributes to global warming. If trees are not replanted, wood heating releases more CO_2 than coal. On top of CO_2, wood combustion releases carbon monoxide, fine dust particles, nitrogen oxides, benzene, organic volatile compounds etc.

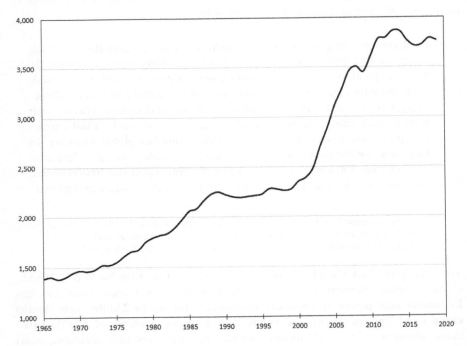

FIGURE 4.6 Evolution of world coal consumption from 1965 to 2019, in millions of toe. (Source: *BP statistical review of world energy 2020*.)

According to Ademe – the French environment and energy management agency – the fine dust particles released by burning wood can increase cardio-pulmonary morbidity, asthma, cardiovascular diseases, lung cancer, chronic airway diseases, arteriosclerosis, birth defects and respiratory illnesses in children. These emissions can certainly be curbed by using recent appliances, but they cannot be annihilated.

The *Airparif* association, who monitors air quality in the Paris area, confirms that "the consumption of firewood contributes by up to 88% to fine dust particle emissions in the residential sector while it only covers 5% of heating energy needs".

In 2014, there were even suggestions to ban open chimney fires in Paris, wood being suspected of contributing to some fine dust particles emissions as much as road transport. At the end of 2015, the Lord Mayor of San Vitaliano, near Naples, even imposed filters meant to curb fine dust particle emissions released by pizza ovens!

According to the European Environment Agency and the World Health Organization, air pollution causes tens of thousands of early deaths in France every year, several hundreds of thousands in Europe and several million worldwide! This pollution is largely due to fine particles and nitrogen oxides released by the combustion of fossil energy sources and wood. A study published in the scientific European Heart Journal in 2019 reads: "calculations show that an annual 434,000 excess mortality rate could be avoided by eliminating emissions due to fossil fuels" [EHJ].

4.3 DANGERS OF NUCLEAR ENERGY

The dangers related to this particular source of energy are generally known to the public better than others.

The nuclear industry generates waste that is dangerous for thousands of years.

The risk of nuclear disasters is definitely looming. Everyone keeps Chernobyl and Fukushima in mind.

Dismantling nuclear power stations is complex.

Operating nuclear power stations has an impact on ecosystems since they release hot water, hence contributing to increases in the temperature of the water of some rivers and seas. The fact is that power stations release 98% of the water they collect. In case of heatwaves, it is for environmental and not safety reasons that reactors releasing too much hot water were eventually shut down.

Nuclear power stations release some radioactive waste in a liquid or gaseous form, but under highly regulated limits. Some chemical waste may also be released: sodium, chlorides and sulphates.

Extracting uranium may cause accidents, as any mining activity.

Nuclear energy can be used to manufacture nuclear bombs.

Figure 4.7 shows the global evolution of nuclear energy production from 1965 to 2019. A drop after the Fukushima disaster appears clearly, followed by a new rise. According to the International Energy Agency, the world nuclear energy capacity is expected to increase by 60% between 2013 and 2040, in China and Russia mainly.

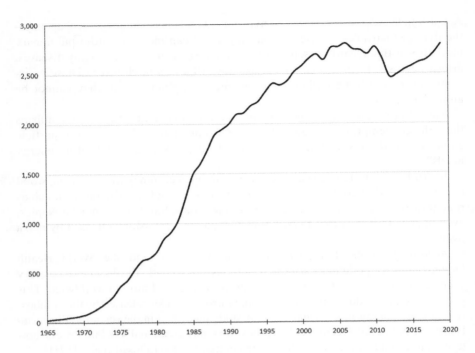

FIGURE 4.7 Evolution of world nuclear energy production from 1965 to 2019, in TWh. (Source: *BP statistical review of world energy 2020.*)

4.4 THE DANGERS OF OTHER RENEWABLE ENERGY SOURCES

Building hydro-power dams modifies ecosystems, provokes the decomposition of the submerged plants and requires populations to be evacuated.

China's Three Gorges Dam, 185 metres high and 2 km long, has a power output of 22,500 MW, which is the equivalent of about no less than 22 nuclear reactors, and required moving 1.8 million people! In France, the construction of dams, such as the ones in Tignes or Serre-Ponçon, was humanly very hard; villages had to be evacuated by force.

Bursts are a definite risk and have occurred several times, as for example:

- Malpasset dam burst in France in 1959 with 423 dead.
- Vajont dam burst in Longarone, in Italy in 1963 with 1,900 dead.
- Macchu-2 dam burst, near Morvi in India in 1979 with between 2,000 and 15,000 dead.
- Banqio dam burst in China in 1975 with at least 100,000 dead.
- Saddle Dam D burst, in Laos, in July 2018 with several dozens of dead.

– Wind turbines have an unpleasant visual and sound impact. They are harmful to certain birds and bats. As with any human construction, the manufacturing, installation and maintenance of wind turbines or solar panels require energy and materials, and generate waste. Wind turbines often use magnets made of rare-earth elements, the extraction of which generates pollution. Photovoltaic panels require lead, cadmium and bromine. These drawbacks may be seen as unimportant compared to the ones involved with other energy sources, but wind turbines and solar panels supply an energy that varies depending on weather conditions and are generally used to produce an energy that is hard to store. To be fair, one should consider the dangers of electricity-producing systems seen in parallel and/or associated with their corresponding storage installations. Battery energy storage, STEP or synthetic gas production is always a complicated and potentially dangerous operation.

Solar energy consumes a lot of surface area, and solar parks should not replace farming areas, meadows or even forests too often. Mega solar parks, such as *Solarzac*, are emerging, and should cover 400 hectares (990 acres) of land in Larzac. In 2019, the project produced a fierce reaction from inhabitants, hunters, farmers and environmentalists who fear land-grabs, impact on birds, water consumption etc.

Moreover, if a wind turbine or a solar panel may be seen as harmless compared to a coal or nuclear power station, the danger is to be considered in proportion to the amount of energy generated.

- Geothermal energy exploits underground heat, i.e. the energy contained in the centre of the Earth. The deeper you go, the higher the temperature. Deep geothermal energy requires complex drillings. It is sometimes considered to have the same drawbacks as hydraulic fracturing: micro-seismic activity, impact on water tables.
- Agrofuels, which exploit agricultural crops – wood, colza, sugar cane etc. – to be turned into fuels, and require large surface areas, are obviously in competition with food and may be an incentive for deforestation.
- Ocean energy, which exploits swell, sea currents or tides, for example, requires the installation at sea of large infrastructures which are obviously likely to disturb ecosystems. Fishermen look unfavourably on the arrival of off-shore wind turbines in their fishing areas. Marine turbines, which are underwater turbines activated by sea currents, create turbulent flow areas which can be detrimental to sedimentation, marine animals and plants. Tidal power-plants modify ecosystems in estuaries.

It is not easy to compare the dangers provoked by the various energy sources because the problems brought out are not always the same. In any case, I consider that dangers and drawbacks should be considered in proportion to the amount of energy produced.

5 A Comparison of Energy Sources: Related Dangers and Issues

Several studies have tried to compare the dangers related to the various electricity-producing energy sources. See below the results of some of these.

5.1 FIGURES FROM INTERGOVERNMENTAL PANEL ON CLIMATE CHANGE EXPERTS [IPCC-III]

The Intergovernmental Panel on Climate Change has obviously looked at the matter of greenhouse gas emissions released by the various electricity-producing systems. In their last report (Appendix III) [IPCC III], they produce the data in Figure 5.1.

It is not surprising that coal, being the electricity-producing energy source mostly used around the world, is therefore responsible for the largest amount of greenhouse gas emissions. Gas, with strong growth in recent years, is not so bad, but its emissions remain enormous in comparison with renewable and nuclear technologies. These technologies do not actually produce any greenhouse gas emissions, but the manufacturing, maintenance and end-of-life treatment (…) of the structures have to be considered. Nuclear energy is at the same level as wind energy, and is responsible for three to four times less greenhouse gas emission than photovoltaic energy. And yet, recent uranium enrichment technologies, now used in France, allow for nuclear energy with half the emissions (6 g CO_2 per kWh). Moreover, we must keep in mind that wind and solar installations only produce energy when wind and/or sunlight are present, controllable power stations or heavy storage systems being then needed, the impact of which is not accounted for. For their part, nuclear installations are controllable and allow production to adapt to demand without needing any additional system. The poor efficiency of biomass is also to be noted while wood power stations are being developed.

Noting from a survey released in 2019 that a majority of the French – 69% – think that nuclear energy contributes to global warming is something that makes you tear your hair out! **The energy sources with the lowest contribution to global warming are wind and nuclear energies.**

5.2 A STUDY CONDUCTED BY FRANZ H. KOCH, HYDROPOWER-INTERNALIZED COSTS AND EXTERNALIZED BENEFITS [KOCH]

This study was carried out by Franz H. Koch from the International Energy Agency. It presents the results from an analysis of the production lifecycle of 1

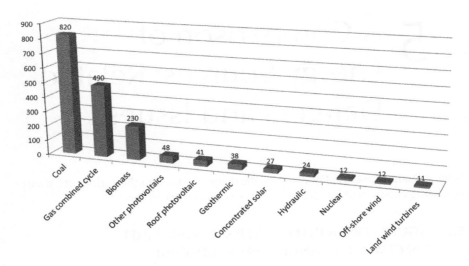

FIGURE 5.1 Greenhouse gas emissions according to electricity production. Median values in gCO$_2$eq/kWh. (From: "Technology-Specific Cost and Performance Parameters", IPCC, 2014 – 5th report – app. 3.)

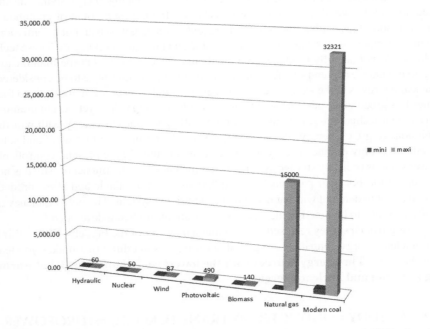

FIGURE 5.2 Sulphur dioxide emissions generated by the production of 1 kWh electricity, in mg per kWh. (From: *Hydropower-Internalized Costs and Externalized Benefits*, Frans H. Koch, International Energy Agency – Implementing Agreement for Hydropower Technologies and Programs, Ottawa, Canada, 2000 [Koch].)

kWh of electricity. Lifecycle analyses are a relatively recent discipline aiming at evaluating the environmental impacts from the extraction of raw materials to the production of waste. The study presented here focuses on the impact of fine dust particles, sulphur dioxide, nitrogen oxides and volatile organic compounds. These choices may obviously be questioned as other criteria might have been taken into account.

Figure 5.2 illustrates sulphur dioxide emissions: coal and gas are clearly the worst sources of pollution. As there are several processes and possible margins of error, minimal and maximal emissions are considered. The photovoltaic process is far from being the least harmful. **Hydraulic, nuclear and wind sources have the lowest impact.**

In Figure 5.3, coal is the definite leader for fine dust particle emissions, followed by wood, the photovoltaic process being the third most polluting. **Nuclear energy would then be the one with the lowest emissions, followed by hydro and then by wind energies.** With this criterion, photovoltaic energy would be responsible for higher pollution than gas. The relative harmfulness of wood is also to be noted.

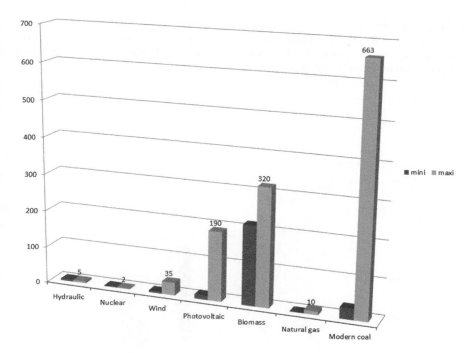

FIGURE 5.3   Fine particle emissions generated by the production of 1 kWh electricity, in mg per kWh. (From: *Hydropower-Internalized Costs and Externalized Benefits*, Frans H. Koch, International Energy Agency – Implementing Agreement for Hydropower Technologies and Programs, Ottawa, Canada, 2000 [Koch].)

60   Energy Transition

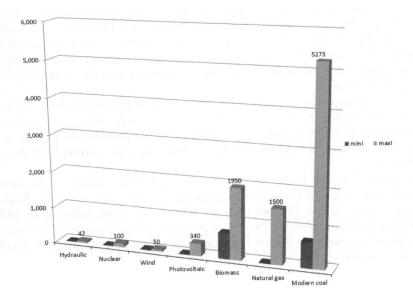

FIGURE 5.4 Nitrogen oxides emissions generated by the production of 1 kWh electricity, in mg/kWh. (From: *Hydropower-Internalized Costs and Externalized Benefits*, Frans H. Koch, International Energy Agency – Implementing Agreement for Hydropower Technologies and Programs, Ottawa, Canada, 2000 [Koch].)

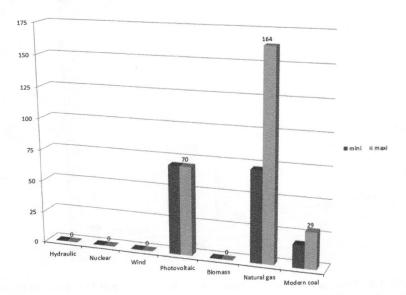

FIGURE 5.5 Non-methanogenic volatile organic compounds emissions generated by the production of 1 kWh of electricity, in mg per kWh. (From: *Hydropower-Internalized Costs and Externalized Benefits*, Frans H. Koch, International Energy Agency – Implementing Agreement for Hydropower Technologies and Programs, Ottawa, Canada, 2000 [Koch].)

The conclusions to be drawn from Figures 5.4 and 5.5 are that **hydraulic, nuclear and wind energies are the least polluting regarding emissions of nitrogen oxide and volatile organic compounds.** Wood combustion is revealed in Figure 5.4 as more polluting than gas consumption. Figure 5.5 concerns volatile organic compound emissions, gas and photovoltaic being the worst.

5.3 A STUDY BY ANIL MARKANDYA AND PAUL WILKINSON, *ELECTRICITY GENERATION AND HEALTH* [MARKANDYA WILKINSON]

The Lancet, in which the study was published, is a reputed British scientific medical review within the scientific community. Anil Markandya is the scientific director at Bilbao's Basque Centre for Climate Change. His work deals with climate change, resources, environment and economy. Paul Wilkinson is a professor in environmental epidemiology at the London School of Hygiene and Tropical Medicine specializing in climate change and pollution effects on health. According to this study,

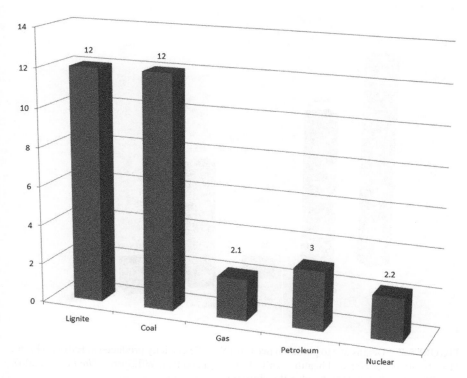

FIGURE 5.6 Fatal accidents per 100 TWh of electricity produced in Europe. (From: "Electricity generation and health", Anil Markandya and Paul Wilkinson, *The Lancet*, 2007, vol. 370, pp. 979–990 [Markandya Wilkinson].)

nuclear energy is the source with the lowest impact on CO_2, before hydroelectricity, wind, solar and biomass, and far ahead of gas, oil and coal.

The authors also focused on accidents, accidental deaths and diseases related to pollution caused by the various energy sources. Mortality was related to the amount of energy produced. Figures 5.6 to 5.8 give the results. Lignite, which is a poor-quality type of coal, appears separately. These energy sources, together with oil, are responsible for the highest rates of deaths and diseases. **Nuclear energy appears as the least harmful of the compared energies**, but it is true that biomass is the only renewable energy to be considered. Of course, this study, dating back to 2007, takes Chernobyl's consequences into account but not Fukushima's, which will not actually result in different orders of magnitude.

According to the figures from this study, the production of electricity would be responsible for 37 deaths per year in France if it were 100% nuclear, 1,410 deaths if 100% produced from gas, 2,315 deaths if 100% produced from biomass, 9,215 from oil and 28,670 if from coal.

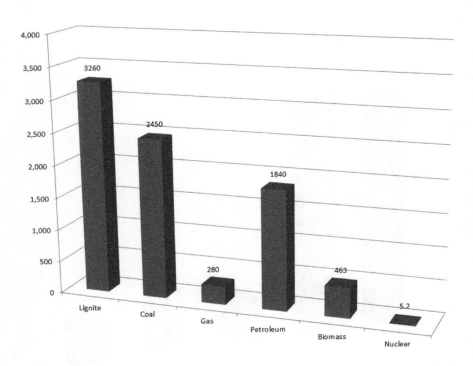

FIGURE 5.7   Deaths due to pollution per 100 TWh of electricity produced in Europe. (From: "Electricity generation and health", Anil Markandya and Paul Wilkinson, *The Lancet*, 2007, vol. 370, pp. 979–990 [Markandya Wilkinson].)

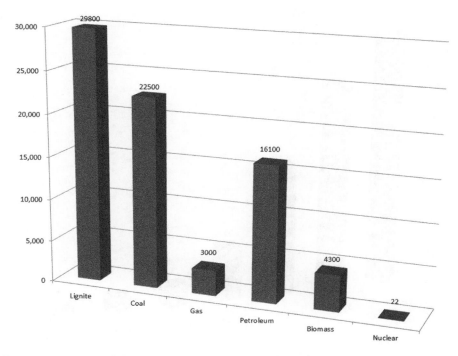

FIGURE 5.8 Serious diseases due to pollution per 100 TWh of electricity produced in Europe. (From: "Electricity generation and health", Anil Markandya and Paul Wilkinson, *The Lancet*, 2007, vol. 370, pp. 979–990 [Markandya Wilkinson].)

5.4 A STUDY BY RABL AND SPADARO, *LES COÛTS EXTERNES DE L'ÉLECTRICITÉ* [RABL SPADARO]

In 2001, the authors published a summary of the European Union's ExternE – external costs of energy – project. This study dealt with the financial costs and damage related to the pollution generated by various electricity production methods. The reduction in life expectancy, expressed in lost years of life per TWh of electricity produced, is shown in Figure 5.9. **Wind energy is the least deadly, followed by nuclear energy.** Fuel-oil, i.e. petroleum, and coal are clearly the most dangerous, although I have only represented the most recent technologies. It used to be worse, obviously.

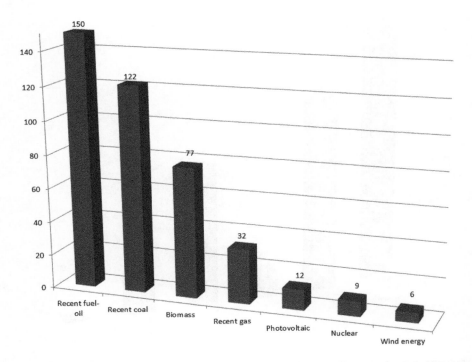

FIGURE 5.9 Number of years of life lost per TWh of electricity produced. (From: A. Rabl & J.V. Spadaro, "Les coûts externes de l'électricité" [Rabl Spadaro].)

5.5   A STUDY CONDUCTED BY KHARECHA AND HANSEN: PREVENTED MORTALITY AND GREENHOUSE GAS EMISSIONS FROM HISTORICAL AND PROJECTED NUCLEAR POWER [KHARECHA HANSEN]

This study was published in 2013 in *Environmental Science & Technology*, a widely recognized scientific review. Its authors, who have accounted for the consequences of the Chernobyl and Fukushima disasters, consider that **nuclear energy has helped avoid 1.8 million deaths** in comparison with electricity production which would have been generated by fossil energies. They also consider that the development of nuclear energy could prevent from about 420,000 to 7 million deaths by the mid-21st century.

I think it is important to highlight the fact that I have not omitted any study with opposing conclusions.

5.6   NUCLEAR ENERGY

The Cartesian, scientific and rational reasoning I am trying to stick to leads to the support of nuclear energy. The matter is so divisive that some readers may get angry with me, accusing me of having a conflict of interest, of being in the terrible nuclear lobby's pay.

I have absolutely no financial interest directly or indirectly in nuclear energy. I am only interested in standing up for my future, and even more so my children's future, as they are likely to have to live in a more challenging world with less available energy. When I was 14 years old, I would wear a "Nuclear? No thanks" campaign badge. When I was 20 years old, I was thinking about the necessity to find something else. Today, I think that no solution comes without drawbacks and that we just have to opt for the least harmful choice.

The drawbacks of nuclear energy [Basdevant], particularly its waste and the risk of a disaster, are real and well known, widely covered by the media. They are often seen as more frightening than a shortage of energy or the impact of fossil fuels. And yet, a shortage of energy is a potential disaster for human beings, and fossil energies are clearly more dangerous.

Radioactivity frightens people, but it does exist in nature, in France and particularly in such popular French areas as the Breton tourist-appealing *Granit Rose* Coast, the green and wooded Massif Central and the Vosges mountains or Corsica. Cosmic rays are radioactive. In nuclear medicine, radioactive products are voluntarily administered to patients. Food stuffs – particularly strawberries – are commonly irradiated for better preservation and to avoid the use of pesticides. Many food products are naturally radioactive: bananas, for example, are sufficiently radioactive to be detected by customs services. Human beings are naturally radioactive, with around 8,000 becquerels in adults.

As a matter of fact, radioactivity is not necessarily harmful. It depends on the type of radiation concerned, and, of course, on its dose. The debate about hazard thresholds shall always be raging, but it seems absurd to me to see radioactivity as hazardous whatever its dose, as some associations do, alarming people by putting forward the fact that a higher than "normal" radioactivity rate has been observed. The level of radioactivity can be largely higher than naturally "normal" without exceeding standards and being a problem. Nuclear energy may obviously be dangerous, but the true question is to know whether it is more or less hazardous than other options. Compared with the typical drawbacks of fossil energies and a looming energy shortage, the benefit-to-risk ratio is likely to be in favour of nuclear.

The type of pollution generated by nuclear waste, when concentrated, wrapped, confined, known about, managed and with a long life span, is preferable to the kind of pollution from fossil energy sources, which is scattered, uncontrolled and with an infinite life span. Mercury, for example, is a poison that is largely released by the combustion of coal. It is eventually to be found in oceans and in the flesh of the fish we eat, and its life span is infinite.

In France, within the scope of the *Cigéo* project, nuclear waste is about to be stored 500 metres underground, in an impermeable argillaceous rock layer chosen for its confinement properties over very long time scales and because of its 150-million-year-long geological stability. I find this solution reasonable and absolutely harmless for the people living in the area. Of course, it does not please antinuclear activists who are hence deprived of their popular argument saying that "nobody knows what to do with nuclear waste".

Fifteen nuclear reactors have been fully dismantled across the world. The reactor of the Maine Yankee Power Plant in the United States, with a 900-MW power, comparable to most French reactors, was dismantled in eight years for a reasonable cost of 500 million dollars. Today, cows are peacefully grazing in the area where the power station used to be and I would drink their milk without fear. It is therefore wrong to claim that the dismantling of nuclear reactors is impossible.

The risk of a new nuclear disaster cannot be completely ruled out in spite of the extensive precautions that are now being taken. There will always be points of controversy about the consequences of the Chernobyl and Fukushima disasters. According to WHO, the Chernobyl disaster was responsible for several thousands of dead [WHO Chernobyl], but coal kills hundreds of thousands of people every year. **Accounting for the number of dead, fossil energies amount to several hundreds of Chernobyl disasters every year!** Radioactive waste due to Fukushima's nuclear disaster will obviously have an impact on health but the WHO website notes that "the expected risks are low for the whole population inside and outside Japan". The report produced in 2013 by the United Nations' Scientific Committee about the effects of ionizing radiation [UNSCEAR][GEO] confirms that "no death or serious disease related to radiation was observed following the Fukushima accident", and that "no perceptible radiation-related consequence is to be expected among the people exposed or their descendants", "the Fukushima accident is responsible for no victim, death or disease due to the radiation emitted and that, in the future, the consequences of this radiation will be too weak to be discernible". This report, written in 2015 by 80 experts from 18 countries, was largely ignored by the media.

Whoever is doubtful about these rather too official information sources can check them on Wikipedia [wiki Fukushima] where it says that 45–55 people died because of the accident or the evacuation from the Fukushima area, not more than 20 people were seriously injured or irradiated, fewer than 1,000 people were slightly injured or irradiated. It is obviously too many, but it is also insignificant compared to the diseases caused by other energy sources.

I will probably be told that these reassuring reports originate from people with conflicts of interest, under the influence of the famous nuclear lobby, and that other reports have conclusions accounting for much more dreadful consequences. But these other reports more often than not originate from antinuclear activists whose objectivity is not to be taken for granted as they endeavour to show the dangers of what they struggle against. Their associations who fight against nuclear energy would lose all interest, hence funding and jobs, if they started confirming official figures.

I think that the figures provided by UNSCEAR and WHO, which are from the United Nations, are the most reliable. As Jean-Marc Jancovici points out, the IPCC also originates from the UN and, apart from some hardliner climate sceptics, few people question these figures. Considering that fossil energy lobbies are unable to stop the IPCC from declaring their harmful effect on climate change, it is rather difficult to imagine how the nuclear lobby, which is far less powerful than the other, would manage to have an important influence on the UN's reports.

Anyway, so serious as they are, the consequences of Fukushima – the evacuation of residents and radioactive pollution – have to be considered in the context of an earthquake and a tsunami which killed no less than 15,000 people and sent tons of various items and pollutants into the sea: cars, household debris, machines, hydrocarbons, solvents, acids, pesticides, medicines and other toxic pollutants, the consequences of which are not quantifiable. By the way, this earthquake provoked the rupture of the Fujinuma hydraulic dam causing several deaths. Several tens of thousands of people died because of hydraulic dam ruptures during the 20th century, but they also killed more people than nuclear accidents, and yet no one calls for the production of hydroelectricity to be stopped.

Around 100,000 people had to be evacuated from the Fukushima area, i.e. less than 20% of the people who lost their homes because of the earthquake and the tsunami. The construction of China's Three-Gorges dam, which is also used to produce electricity, caused the evacuation of more than ten times as many people as the Fukushima nuclear power station. The evacuated area is 370 km^2, while the exploitation of opencast coal mines in Germany destroyed more than 500 km^2 of countryside.

After the disaster, Japan shut down its nuclear power stations which produced 28% of Japanese electricity. This lack of production was very marginally compensated for by electricity savings but largely by increased gas, fuel-oil and coal-produced electricity, which involved emissions of CO_2 and various pollutants [Livet]. The proportion of coal in the production of Japanese electricity went up from 27 to 33% and gas from 28 to 39% between 2010 and 2015 while consumption dropped just by 10%. It is highly probable that the consequences of these emissions on health are going to be worse than the impact of radioactivity following the Fukushima accident. Bernard Durand is a fossil-fuel geochemist, the former director of the Geology-Geochemistry unit of *Institut Français du Pétrole et des Énergies Nouvelles* and former head of *École Normale Supérieure de Géologie*. In 2018, he explained that "on a planetary scale, air pollution represents a mortality risk about ten times as high as radioactivity, including the contribution of Chernobyl and Fukushima", and that

> we observe that living for 50 years in Paris, where fine dust particles are permanently as high as 50 µg PM 2.5 per m^3, i.e., currently, in places located by the main highways, is more risky than living for 50 years in the Fukushima areas where 50-mSv radioactivity doses are currently received every year and which were consequently evacuated.
>
> **[Durand]**

A parallel can be drawn with a comparison between transport means: aircraft are more frightening than others because air disasters are spectacular, but they are the safest of all, statistically.

The countries which are currently managing to produce electricity from sources other than polluting fossil energies are the ones that have developed nuclear power and/or are lucky to have geographic characteristics allowing for hydro-electricity, such as France, Switzerland, Sweden, Norway, Iceland, Austria, Brazil and Canada [Mix]. According to some people, the collapse of our societies is inevitable in the years to come. Human beings would not then be able to manage nuclear power stations, which would become an enormously looming danger. An oil shortage, for example, would make it impossible to use the civil engineering machines required for the construction, maintenance and dismantling of nuclear power stations. Society might even be so disorganized that the management of all this would be made impossible. I have not reached the point of such pessimism. I think the most important thing is to have some energy available to avoid the collapse of our society, the required construction machinery eventually running on the electricity produced by the power stations. I think that, in France, this industry is more closely watched than any other [Barré] [Kuo], particularly by the *Autorité de Sûreté Nucléaire* – the nuclear safety authority – whose commissioners are indefeasible for the six years of their mandates, are reputed to be strict and are granted the authority to shut down a power station. The nuclear industry is also under the careful watch of antinuclear associations who never miss an opportunity to broadcast stressful messages when the slightest dysfunction occurs, supported by the media who love to relay them with shocking headlines meant to generate a maximum number of clicks on the web. For example, in July 2019, the *Association pour le Contrôle de la Radioactivité* – the radioactivity control association – in Western France, which has several employees, gave an alarm concerning the presence of tritium – a radioactive element – in river waters and in the drinking water network supplying millions of people. Their stressful messages were taken into account by the *Commission de Recherche et d'Information Indépendantes sur la Radioactivité*, (CRIIRAD, a commission in charge of independent research and information about radioactivity employing 14 wage earners) and by the media. The highest value mentioned, 341 Bq/L, was 29 times lower than the drinking water threshold set by WHO (10,000 Bq/L). People would have had to drink at least 40 litres of water to receive the amount of radioactivity contained in one banana! The press did a good job mentioning that the levels recorded were extremely low, but the damage had been done: crazy rumours had spread, thousands of people refused to drink tap water, which contributed to the addition of more lorries on the road to transport plastic bottles.

Brice Lalonde, an environmentalist and an Environment Minister from 1988 to 1992, declared in the newspaper *La Voix du Nord* in January 2016:

> I would like to appeal to ecologists to take into account that nuclear energy releases no CO2 emissions and is safe in our countries. I used to be a fierce antinuclear activist, but this technology should not be banned when an energy transition towards a clean energy is to be implemented urgently.

Patrick Moore, a founder of Greenpeace, admitted, in the German daily *Die Welt* in 2008: "Today, I am absolutely convinced that the campaign against nuclear energy was stupid. We were wrong to tar with the same bush nuclear weapons and nuclear energy, as if anything nuclear were bad". The confusion between civil nuclear and military nuclear is actually kept alive by some people. Very few technologies would be used if the ones used by armies were to be banned!

Of course, nuclear energy does not account for a large part of the world's energy currently – about 2% of final energy – but it does better than wind or solar energy

– about 1% and 0.5% – but it is no indication of the part these technologies might play in the future.

In my opinion, there will be fewer problems with nuclear energy than without it. Out of the 1,200 scenarios recorded by IPPC, only 8 claim that global warming could be limited to 2°C without using nuclear energy. The International Energy Agency estimates that, since 1971, the use of nuclear energy has avoided an equivalent of a two-year amount of the world current CO_2 emissions [WEO]. In a report published in May 2019 [IEA nuclear power], the International Energy Agency recommends an 80% increase of the world production of nuclear energy by 2040 and expresses concerns about a decline of nuclear power: "without an investment in nuclear energy, a sustainable energy system will be a lot more difficult to implement",

> in case no complementary investment is provided for by advanced economies in order to extend the lifespan of existing nuclear power stations or develop new projects … gas and coal, to a lesser extent, would play an important role to replace nuclear energy. Total CO2 emissions would rise by 4 billion tons by 2040, which would only make emission objectives even more difficult to meet.

However, I would not claim that nuclear energy is free from any drawback or that it will be the magic remedy to the energy issue. It would certainly be better to use neither any fossil nor nuclear energy, but only renewable ones. Is it possible? The following developments might help form an opinion.

6 Energy Resources

6.1 FOSSIL RESOURCES

Let us say it again: 80% of the energy consumed across the world is from a fossil origin, i.e. drawn from a stock which cannot be renewed while needs keep increasing. More energy has to be made available year after year, which means that more oil or gas has to be extracted than the year before. It is obvious that this headlong rush will have to stop one day. We may well think that the shortage will not occur for a long time, but it is clear that it will happen.

Wondering in which year this will happen is just a bad question. Actually, this question implies that production will stop suddenly. The reality is probably far more complex, depending on the evolution of techniques, the discovery of new pools or deposits more or less difficult to exploit, the variation of prices and economic crises. Production is most likely to reach a maximum, then stagnate before dwindling. How the maximum phase will take place is the matter of numerous theories and debates. In the 1940s, geophysicist Marion King Hubbert was the first to suggest a bell-shaped curve with a peak of consumption, called "Hubbert peak".

– Concerning oil, some think that the peak has already been or is being reached. Others, being more optimistic, are only expecting it in a few years' time, particularly thanks to hydraulically fracked shale oil, which involves the use of controversial techniques. In any case, almost nobody claims that crude oil may still be abundant by the end of this century. For sure, the conventional oil peak is now behind us. Production is kept steady thanks to non-conventional oils such as bituminous sands and shales or extra heavy oils. The peak of discoveries is also behind us. We currently discover fewer crude oil pools each year than our consumption requires. Even oil companies do not deny that supply issues are getting close. Michel Mallet, director of Total Germany, said in 2009: "in the future, we shall have to invest more just to maintain our current production". Christophe de Margerie, Total's CEO, in the newspaper *Le Monde* in 2013, stated that because of our limited capacities to transform oil resources, "the oil-production level should begin to reach a ceiling around 2020–2025". Peter Voser, Shell's CEO, stated in 2011 that

> the production from existing fields is declining by 5% per year as resources run dry, so much so that the world should add the equivalent of four Saudi Arabias or ten North-Seas within the ten years to come, just to maintain supply at its current level, even before any demand increase.

Along the same lines, Patrick Pouyanné, Total's CEO, declared in the newspaper *Le Monde* in 2018 that "after 2020, we are likely to run out of oil" and in 2019, in *Le Journal du Dimanche*, that "within twenty years, the oil market should start decreasing". The International Energy Agency, for its part, stated that "throughout the last three years, the number of conventional oil production approved new projects only accounts for half of the volume required to balance the market until 2025".

I would like to encourage you to read *La Vie Après le Pétrole* (Life After Petroleum), a book by Jean-Luc Wingert [Wingert], *Pétrole Apocalypse* by Yves Cochet [Cochet], *The Party's Over: Oil, War, and the Fate of Industrial Societies* by Richad Heinberg [Heinberg], *Le plein, s'il vous plait* (Fill up, please) by Jean-Marc Jancovici [Jancovici Le Plein] or *Oil, Power and War: A Dark History* by Mathieu Auzanneau [Auzanneau]. There is nothing joyful about these works: their authors all think that the abundant petroleum era will not last and that the consequences will be huge.

Maarten Van Mourik and Oscar Slingerland, two petroleum company executives, explained in 2014 that "in the end, there is nowhere in the world any substantial amount of oil that can be still exploited rapidly at a low cost", "everything tells us that we are closer than ever to the limits of a maximum oil production capacity" [Mourik].

Philippe Charlez, a rock mechanics expert for Total, specializing in non-conventional resources, wrote, in 2017, that "despite an apparent abundance in non-conventional resources, fossil fuels are getting more and more difficult to exploit, hence to produce", "peaks are about a few dozens of years away, barely more" [Charlez].

The French specialist, Mathieu Auzanneau, declared in August 2019:

The International Energy Agency considers that the only way to maintain the production of oil is to exploit the American shale oil. It is a currently booming industry but showing more and more signs of technical and financial weaknesses, which seems to rule out any doubling or trebling of this output, which is nevertheless necessary to compensate for the lack of conventional oil.

- Natural gas reserves would be slightly larger than those of oil, but its consumption is rising sharply (Figure 4.5). France refuses to exploit shale gas in its territory for very understandable environmental reasons, but, according to the multinational companies' observations, France is thought to have imported American shale gas transported by tankers from America. The French attitude is therefore quite hypocritical.
- Unfortunately, coal reserves seem to be in a better situation. As you have obviously realized, coal is by far the most polluting, harmful and dangerous energy source of all. It is used a lot for the production of electricity but might also be used as a motor-car fuel one day. We know how to produce a type of synthetic petrol from coal, a process that had already been used during the Second World War to make up for the Wehrmacht's shortage in oil, and, of course, a very polluting process too. With energy requirements increasing with the growing world population and the development of poor countries, coal is very much likely to remain an important energy source in spite of pollution, global warming and the promises of the authorities who are disarmed by the complexity of the issues.

As fossil resources dwindle, we have to get them from further and further away, which means more labour, more materials and particularly more energy are necessary. Energy for energy! In Canada, one oil barrel is consumed to extract three or four barrels of bituminous sand oil. We shall come back to this point later on.

6.2   RESOURCES FOR NUCLEAR ENERGY

Einstein established the famous relation $E = mc^2$, which means that the amount of energy – E – that matter possesses equals its mass – m – multiplied by the speed of light squared – c^2. The energy of atoms is considerable because the speed of light is very high (300,000 km/sec). So, my pen, which only weighs 10 grams, possesses a potential energy of 900 million million joules, i.e. 250,000 million Wh, which is the energy needed to supply about 80,000 homes for one year! It is just amazing! Yet, nuclear fission, which allows the release of the energy of atoms constituting matter, is only achieved with uranium currently, and the fission of a uranium core only releases about a thousandth of the energy contained in its mass, which is already considerable. One day, in the distant future, we might be able to extract energy from any atom.

According to the International Atomic Energy Agency, the world's identified uranium resources featuring a reasonable extraction cost account for the equivalent of a century-long consumption at the current pace. They are mainly located in Australia – 31% of proven reserves – and in Kazakhstan, Canada, Russia, Nigeria, South Africa, Brazil and Namibia. Of course, if nuclear energy was to be developed on a broad scale with the aim of replacing fossil energies, resources would then dwindle rapidly. But other deposits exist: uranium is found, in low concentrations, everywhere in the Earth's crust and even in sea water. The world's oceans contain, in a dissolved form, enough to supply our existing power stations for as long as tens of thousands of years! Moreover, there is not just one way of producing energy from atoms. New types of reactors, fast-neutron reactors, called "generation-4 reactors", could emerge. The fourth generation could be supplied with uranium-238, which is a hundred times as abundant as uranium-235 currently in use, or with thorium, which is four times as abundant as uranium. The use of these technologies would allow for several thousands of years of reserves, a time scale that makes them equal to renewable energies! It is no science-fiction. Several types of generation-4 reactors are being studied in South Africa, Argentina, Brazil, Canada, China, South Korea, the United States, France, Japan, the United Kingdom, Russia and Switzerland.

In France, the project was called Astrid. It was inspired by the breeder reactors Phenix and Superphenix, which have now been closed down. They were a matter of controversy and far from being perfect, but they worked. Unfortunately, the project does not seem to be likely to see the light of day. Uranium is currently so broadly available and cheap that there is no urgent need for this type of reactor, and France decided to stop the project in 2019. Yet, Russia started an 800-MW fast-neutron reactor in 2016. It has now been connected to the network and seems to be working well, and a 1200-MW reactor is being developed. France might regret its choice within a few years if nuclear energy develops across the world and uranium resources happen to run out. This scenario seems to me very likely. When oil and gas run out, when states have realized that renewable energies cannot be sufficient, many will probably turn to nuclear energy. Let us hope, at least, that the know-how in this field will not be completely lost.

Nuclear fusion is yet another very different technology that might emerge some time in the future. It roughly consists in reproducing the reactions occurring at the surface of the sun. The construction of the international ITER project is underway in France.

6.3   RENEWABLE RESOURCES

Assessing the whole potential of renewable power around the world is a very difficult operation. The Earth receives around 8,000 times as much energy from the sun as human beings consume [Ben Ahmed], which incites some people to say that renewable energy sources can obviously cover human needs. To me, this reasoning is a little too simple because harnessing, concentrating, storing and transporting renewable energies, which are scattered by nature, are very complex processes. Human activities have soared thanks to fossil energy sources which are, in contrast, very much concentrated.

– Solar energy: harnessing solar energy requires space, as the solar radiation received is directly proportional to the surface area. More than 71% of the planet's surface is covered by oceans on top of which it is difficult to imagine installing solar panels. On land, they must not disturb plants. Photosynthesis would obviously be hampered under solar panels which would absorb the solar energy required by vegetation. The amount of potential appropriate places is consequently considerably reduced.

Fallow lands and industrial wastelands can probably be used to install photovoltaic panels. If we forget about the huge transport and storage problems, 5,000 km^2 would be necessary to produce the electricity France needs, and just to mention electricity among other types of energy. It means that about the surface area of a French *département* would have to be made available and on which plants would no longer grow normally. Four times as much would be needed to supply all the energy France requires.

Hence, the idea of putting panels where there is no more vegetation, i.e. on roofs. In France, every square metre receives a little more than 1,200 kWh per year from the sun. A photovoltaic panel with about a 10% yield thus produces a little more than 120 kWh per square metre per year. There are about 30 million homes in France, which means fewer than 30 million roofs, since there are collective dwelling buildings. But there are factory, shop and office building roofs. Not all of them are facing south, which is the favourite orientation for solar energy, and some roofs are in the shade of buildings or include obstacles such as chimneys or windows. So, I think that keeping this estimate is rather optimistic. Installing 20 m^2 of solar panels on each roof would involve a huge amount of work for many years, requiring a lot of skilled staff, the manufacturing of millions of panels and inverters and the adaptation of the electricity network. Such a configuration would produce 60 TWh, i.e. 14% of the consumption of electricity or 3% of the consumption of energy in France.

In any case, as the sun does not always shine, gigantic storage systems would have to be developed. As storage and transmission inevitably involve considerable losses, available final energy would be far lower. As solar panel technology is admittedly progressing, their yield could improve. Solar walls and roadways are definitely envisaged. But in spite of all this, these improvements will not change the orders of magnitude much. It will remain difficult to rely heavily on solar energy.

The production of solar energy may be relevant in the Sahara where large sunny areas are available and on which the presence of panels would not be harmful to vegetation. The 2003 Désertec project was based on this idea: a huge project planning to exploit the deserts in North Africa and the Middle-East in order to provide the neighbouring regions and even Europe with electricity. Large companies were involved, but the project was abandoned in 2014 due to its cost, particularly because of the huge transmission lines that would have had to be constructed.

This does not mean that deserts will not be used to exploit solar energy. Noor, the thermodynamic solar power station installed in Ouarzazate in south Morocco, is working and should eventually be the world's largest solar power station with a power of 580 MW – 580 million watts – i.e. roughly half the power of a nuclear reactor. With more power stations, Morocco is planning a huge 2,000-MW solar electric power. These projects are all the more interesting as the concentrated solar power technology – non-photovoltaic – is a solution to keep producing electricity for a few hours after sunset, which reduces the need for storage. I support these projects. However, with the following developments, I may be seen as a killjoy.

- Water is required to clean and cool panels, which is a problem in a desert.
- The electric power set up by the Moroccans is sometimes over 6,000 MW and not necessarily at a time when power stations supply their maximum power.
- Morocco's energy consumption increases by 4–6% per year.
- Solar energy production will drop a few hours after sunset while many lights will still be on and electric appliances working.
- Just one nuclear reactor has a power of over 1,000 MW and covers a surface area of less than 1 km^2 while the Noor installation will require 25 km^2 for just 580-MW.
- A 1,386-MW (!) mega-coal-plant was brought into operation in 2018 in Safi, near Casablanca, and another 1,320-MW plant is being planned for 2021 in North Morocco within the project of the new Nador West Med harbour. It is much less mentioned in the newspapers these days.

Let us keep in mind that, in France, although nuclear energy is often said to have hindered the development of renewable energy sources, the Themis solar power station in the Pyrenees was one of the first concentrated solar power stations as early as in 1983.

According to Philippe Bihouix who wrote *L'Âge des low-tech* [Bihouix low tech], to produce the whole world's electricity consumption, i.e. one-fifth of the energy consumed, given the production capacity of the factories manufacturing panels, the number of solar panels to be installed would be the equivalent of 500 years of current production!

Nevertheless, I think that some technologies exploiting solar energy are underused. Thermal solar energy facilitates the heating of water and homes without relying on electricity. In some of the hottest countries, they just put a black tank on house roofs to get hot water. It works in the summer under some latitudes, but if we wanted to rely on it in France, we would require a more advanced, unfortunately expensive and very little subsidized technology. These technologies, which would result in saving substantial amounts of gas or fuel-oil, hence CO_2 emissions and pollutants, are thus being developed very slowly. Besides, I think that passive solar energy is far too poorly accounted for in the way homes are designed. Basically, it would mean placing home windows facing south in order to benefit from a maximum of solar rays, hence reducing the needs in heating. It is a simple yet efficient solution.

– Biomass exploits energy from plants, thus solar energy through photosynthesis which miraculously stores the energy from the sun, transforming CO_2 into organic matter. Biomass includes wood, biofuels and biogas. Its potential is limited by the renewal of forests and the fact that fields must be primarily used to feed us. Wood heating has been used forever. Wood heating is not available to everybody since resorting to biomass intensively would result in deforestation and soil erosion. Wood is only renewable if we let forests grow back, which takes time. It has been common in past centuries for humans to deforest certain areas far too much. This was the case in the Serre-Chevalier valley near Briançon (France) for example, where people had to turn to coal as early as in the 17th century because forests had been overexploited.

According to Jean-Marc Jancovici, [Jancovici Web], heating the whole country of France with firewood would require exploiting 20–25% of the country's forests. The wood-fired power station in Gardanne, in Bouches-du-Rhône (France), was built to contribute to reaching 23% renewable energy in France by 2020. But its supply in wood would imply collecting 35% of the forest wealth available in a radius of 250 km and even importing firewood from Canada and Ukraine. In 2015, the Lubéron and Verdon regional parks (in France), together with two local council communities, filed a plea before the administrative court against its exploitation authorization, fearing an excessive need of the local forest resources.

People also fear the impact of truck rotations to supply the power station and the resulting air-pollution by fine dust particles, dioxins and CO_2. The court cancelled the authorization in June 2017. As a result, environment conservation organizations – two regional parks – contributed to hampering the use of a renewable energy. In 2019, a group of environmentalists actually took legal action against the European Union to prevent forest biomass from being included in the directive aiming at reaching 32% of renewable energy by 2030.

If, in France, half of the oil used for transport systems was to be replaced by biofuels, it would require 1.5 times the surface area currently used to grow wheat, 18 times that used to grow rape, 13 times the surface used for sunflower or 16 times that in use for beetroot, according to Pr. J. Foos [Foos].

- It seems to me that biogas is more pertinent, since it uses the fermentation of waste which would have released CO_2 if it was left decomposing in the open air. Instead of this, methane is produced that can be injected into classical gas networks or used to produce electricity. But its potential is limited and its development often hindered by neighbouring residents as they probably baselessly fear a bad smell from methanization installations.
- Wind energy actually exploits solar energy too. Wind is produced by differences in temperature and pressure induced by solar radiation. It requires appropriate sites, which must obviously be windy, but also accessible to construction and maintenance machinery and located far enough from houses and bird migration routes. Moreover, because the wind is lower behind a wind turbine, they cannot be installed too close to one another. Wind turbines at sea are a solution to exploit winds that are stronger and steadier than on land, but they are more difficult to develop. Floating wind turbines are being designed but they are currently tethered to the sea floor, which requires shallow depths of 40 metres maximum, limiting the number of appropriate sites. In France, if we forget about intermittency and storage issues, so essential as they may be, no less than 500,000 2-MW wind turbines would be needed to produce the French energy requirement, which means about 5,000 of them in each *département*, or about a quarter of this if we just refer to electricity and not to all kinds of energy. If one 2-MW wind turbine was installed every 200 metres down from Dunkirk to Biarritz, i.e. some 5,000 wind turbines, they would altogether produce 20 TWh, i.e. less than 5% of the electricity or 1% of the total energy consumed in France. This does not mean that wind energy does not have a role to play. The wind turbines produced nowadays are more and more powerful. Yet, the role this type of energy will play in the future is impaired by such problems as intermittence, storage and electric network stability, constant voltage and frequency being difficult to obtain due to wind variability.

Nobody is likely to envisage French energy as being solely supplied by wind turbines or photovoltaic panels but these simple calculations help us realize what orders of magnitude are likely. Let us bear in mind that these types of non-controllable electrical energy, whether wind or solar, are currently complementing but not replacing other production methods. No storage infrastructures are currently being developed, and there is no incentive towards any deferring of consumption. Therefore, traditional power stations remain necessary though used less. Under these conditions, the relevance of their development may be questioned, as their manufacturing, installation, maintenance and recycling have an environmental impact. Wouldn't the mobilized material and human means be better invested in solar thermal systems, home insulation or public transport?

- Actually, hydroelectricity also exploits solar energy which helps water evaporate causing rain. It still has a big potential on a global scale if people agree to build dams, which means they agree to disturb ecosystems, to

    drown valleys and move local populations etc. In France, it is estimated that the maximum has been reached. Only micro-hydraulic energy production is still being developed despite its low power.
- Ocean energy sources exploit the energy produced by waves, tides and sea currents, i.e. the solar energy creating these movements or the revolution of the moon around the Earth creating tides. The potential of these sources of energy may be high, but their dispersion and the complexity of the techniques to be implemented hinder their development. In France, the Rance tidal power-plant, which exploits the power of tidal movements, remained the world's largest from 1966 to 2011, with a 240-MW capacity. The dam modified the ecosystem considerably and provoked important silting. There are few similar projects around the world, and this source of energy is not likely to play an important part in the future.
- Other renewable energy sources exist. Geothermal energy exploits the heat underground. Cold water can be injected into the underground and the hot water coming back out can be exploited. It is a promising technology, yet developing very slowly.

With heat pumps, which work on the same principle as refrigerators, calories can be transferred from the underground, water tables or ambient air. They consume electricity but far less than classical heating systems, yet they are developing too slowly.

    I would not assert that renewable energy sources have no interest or future. On the contrary, I do consider developing solar thermal energy, concentrated solar power, heat pumps, biogas, etc., as definitely pertinent. But relying on these energy sources even only to maintain our current consumption level seems extremely optimistic.

    We shall see that **no French energy-transition scenario would claim to replace fossil and nuclear energy sources by renewable ones without implying a drastic drop in consumption.** In 2013, ADEME – the environment and energy management agency – published scenarios [Ademe 2013] in which they show "a maximum exploitation of renewable energy potentials" with a total amount accounting for 72.6 Mtoe, a figure that is obtained by simply adding up the data from the documents on page 32 of the document, i.e. 844 TWh of primary energy. Let us keep in mind that 2018's French consumption was about 3,000 TWh for primary energy and 1,800 TWh for final energy.

6.4 ENERGY RETURNED ON ENERGY INVESTED (EROEI)

This coefficient quantifies the amount of energy retrieved, also called "net energy", compared to that used to obtain it. Indeed, energy is required to extract oil, gas or coal, to build and exploit nuclear power stations, wind turbines or photovoltaic panels and to drive the tractors for the production of biofuels.

    Some people sometimes say that both nuclear and renewables could not exist without oil, since their construction, maintenance, dismantling etc. require trucks, excavators, cranes and other equipment powered by oil. Oil is very practical, but these machine engines could be supplied by electrical batteries, synthetic gas or hydrogen coming from the electricity produced, to compressed air obtained thanks to electricity again. Their autonomy would be lower but it is possible, providing that there is enough electricity, i.e. energy available. It is thus fundamental to take the energy returned on energy invested rate into account.

Victor Court, a French economist, gives a very good summary of the importance of EROEI: in the same way as "a predator needs to get, from a prey it consumes, many more calories than it has spent to catch it",

> because they used to generate sufficient energy surpluses thanks to an adequate efficiency – i.e. spending as little time as possible –, our ancestors could devote the time they had left to the construction of their shelters, to the improvement of their camps organization, the protection of their peers, to socialising, to education or else to care for their children and to story-telling.

> The dissipation, i.e. consumption, of energy for the highest needs, such as the achievement of social services and, ultimately, of arts, is only considered as a societal energy necessity once all the lower needs have been at least partly satisfied.

"The access to a 'higher' energy need requires the energy source used to generate an adequate energy surplus" [Court].

A source of energy is only interesting to human beings if its EROEI is higher than one, which means the energy gained is higher than that spent to obtain it. Given the inevitable losses and the necessary infrastructure, an EROEI of 5 would be required for proper access to food; 7 for housing; 10 for an education system; 12 for a healthcare system; and 14 for access to culture and recreation [Thévard]. For good living conditions, it is absolutely necessary to benefit from energy sources with a high EROEI. The economists, Victor Court and Florian Fizaine, have shown that a minimum EROEI of 11 is required for a positive growth rate [Fizaine]. According to researcher Jacques Treiner, the average EROEI of a current energy system is around 10 to 15 [Treiner SPS].

Petroleum EROEI was over 100 in the 19th century, while it is down to less than 20 nowadays, and even 4 for the oil extracted from bituminous sands. "An increase in non-conventional fossil fuels with low EROEI – extra heavy oil, bituminous sands, source-rock oil, etc. – has been observed in the total supply" [Court]. This important evolution should be a serious concern to the people who think that still-abundant oil reserves can keep being exploited and that it is just a matter of money, as exploiting certain energy resources will require so much energy that they will be of no interest at all. Human beings naturally started to look for the easiest reserves to exploit, in other words the reserves requiring the lowest energy. Even with constant production, the net energy available for human activities drops when their EROEI gets lower.

The energy returned on energy invested rate of biofuels is just over 1, according to all studies, which means it is clearly too low for them to be of interest. There is as much fuel spent by tractors, lorries transporting crop and factories transforming biofuels as can be collected in the end. Using biofuels featuring an EROEI inferior to 1 thus means being back to consuming oil reserves and aggravating global warming!

There is no consensus on the way to calculate EROEI, which means that the results obtained differ widely. The differences in these estimations are so important that I have given up on trying to get a synthesis of the averages computed by various authors. I will confine myself to presenting – see Figure 6.1 – the EROEIs of the various electricity production techniques published in two scientific articles. One was written by the English and Italian university lecturers, Marco Raugei and Enrica Lecisi [Raugei], the other by the German D. Weissbach and other Polish, German and Canadian researchers [Weissbach]. The first article concerns the United Kingdom, and the second one includes electricity storage issues.

Large differences can be observed between the two studies related to nuclear energy, coal and gas. The bad score for coal in the United Kingdom is mainly explained by long-distance transport. As for nuclear energy, a very contentious subject, the figures obtained in these two studies are 30 and 75, while they range from 5 to 100 in other works. According to these two publications but also to several other authors, hydroelectric energy has a very good EROEI. Therefore, this renewable energy source features this extra advantage on top of the possibility to store energy by pumping water.

The photovoltaic solar energy EROEI is very poor, according to these two publications – 1.6 and 3.3. It is inferior to 10 in all the studies I could read, and it is even lower if the impact of the often necessary storage of the energy produced is

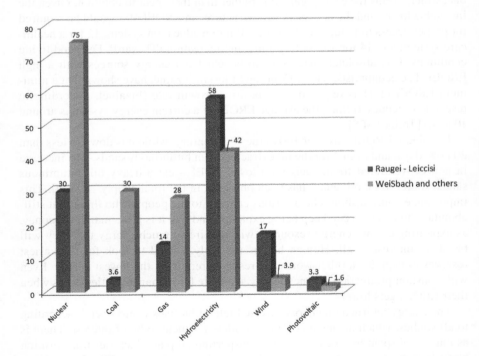

FIGURE 6.1   EROEI of various electricity production techniques according to [Raugei] and [Weissbach].

taken into account. "Between 2000 and 2009, the growth rate of photovoltaic energy throughout the world was 35%, which means that the photovoltaic sector, as with the wind energy sector, consumed much more energy – mainly fossil – than it made available to society" [Thévard]. On top of that, if photovoltaic panels, which have a limited lifespan, are manufactured by Chinese factories using electricity produced from coal containing more than 550 g CO_2 per kWh, then the photovoltaic carbon balance is more than questionable. "Renewable energy sources cannot – at least for the time being – supply as much net energy as we have been used to getting from fossil energy" [Court].

To me, the returned energy rate question is extremely important and largely underestimated in many debates about energy very quickly focusing on money matters while physical matters should come first. Such a technique as biofuels can be interesting financially for those who exploit it by means of a complex system of taxes and subsidies without benefitting human beings.

6.5 THE PROBLEM WITH OTHER RESOURCES

The finitude of the planet's resources is a problem that does not only concern energy. Our rich societies need land, water, sand but also iron ore, aluminium, cement, resins, neodymium, indium, selenium, lithium, etc. Using these mined resources requires energy, ores are required to build energy infrastructures. We have logically exploited the easiest ore deposits, in other words those requiring the least energy. More and more energy is thus necessary to get these resources while non-fossil energies require more metals and other resources than fossil energies. "Metals are necessary to harness, convert and exploit renewable energies. As they are less concentrated and more intermittent, they produce fewer kWhs per mobilised metal unit (copper, steel) than fossil sources" [Bihouix myth]. Recycling is amongst our objectives nowadays as it saves mining resources, but separating the various components of our appliances is a complex and often energy-hungry process! "To produce, store and transport electricity, even the 'green' electricity, many metals are required. Yet, there is no Moore's law – postulating the doubling of the density of transistors every two years or so – in the physical world of energy" [Bihouix myth].

In a report released in June 2017 [World Bank], the World Bank explains that wind and solar energies, and their storage using batteries, require a significantly higher amount of resources than the systems based on fossil energy sources. The demand in metals might double with the development of wind and solar energies. The storage of energy using batteries might increase the demand for lithium by 1,000%! The limitation of the rise of the planet's temperature to 2°C could involve the doubling, or worse, of the demand in aluminium, chromium, copper, indium, iron, lead, nickel, silver, zinc, platinum, neodymium, manganese, etc.

Olivier Vidal's works give a good illustration of the issue. This Frenchman, a research director, specializes in the modelling of interactions between raw materials and energy. He has particularly focused on basic materials such as concrete, steel, aluminium and copper, which cannot be replaced. In his book, *Mineral Resources and Energy* [Vidal], he takes stock of the raw materials required for various electricity production methods. He considers that the potential shortage in the future does not only concern rare metals, which are the subject of careful attention, but also common metals. Figures 6.2 to 6.5, plotted from his numbers, give the quantities of concrete, steel, aluminum and copper required to produce a certain quantity of electrical energy. The author distinguishes various types of photovoltaic solar energy depending on whether panels are installed on roofs, on the ground or in an optimized way with sun-tracking mechanisms. He also distinguishes the concentrated solar energy, which produces electricity without using photovoltaic technology but by heating a heat-transfer fluid.

It is thus clear that exploiting renewable energies uses much more material than fossil and nuclear energies. Olivier Vidal explains that "for an equivalent installed power, solar and wind-power installations require up to 15 times as much concrete, 90 times as much aluminium and 50 times as much iron, copper and glass than fossil and nuclear energies", "by 2050, the world's current production of steel will have to be six or seven times as large just for the renewable energy sector", and that the transfer to renewable energy will replace non-renewable resources (fossil energy sources) by other metals and ores. He also observes that as ores become scarce more energy will be required to extract them!

Guillaume Pitron, a journalist specialising in raw materials geopolitics, explains that energy transition consumes a lot of rare metals used in wind turbines, photovoltaic panels and electric motors and their consumption is bound to soar. In his book *The War of Rare Metals* [Pitron], he maintains that more and more energy is needed to dig them up, that the production of these metals currently

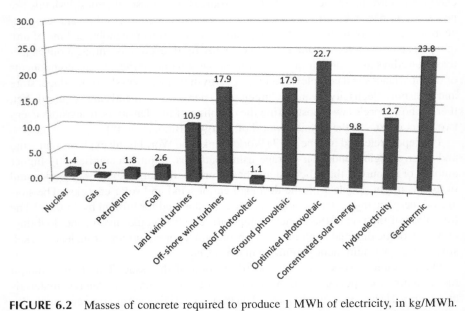

FIGURE 6.2 Masses of concrete required to produce 1 MWh of electricity, in kg/MWh. (From: Olivier Vidal, *Mineral Resources and Energy*, Chapter 5 "Average Material Intensity for Various Modes of Electricity Production", Elsevier, 2018, pp. 69–80.)

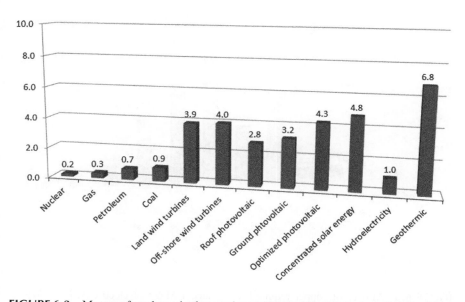

FIGURE 6.3 Masses of steel required to produce 1 MWh of electricity, in kg/MWh. (From: Olivier Vidal, *Mineral Resources and Energy*, Chapter 5 "Average Material Intensity for Various Modes of Electricity Production", Elsevier, 2018, pp. 69–80.)

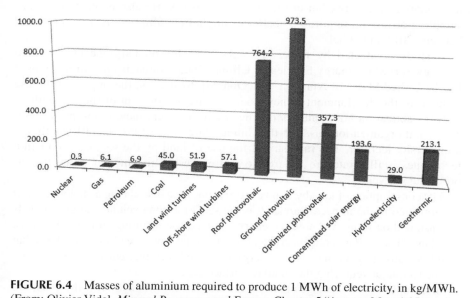

FIGURE 6.4 Masses of aluminium required to produce 1 MWh of electricity, in kg/MWh. (From: Olivier Vidal, *Mineral Resources and Energy*, Chapter 5 "Average Material Intensity for Various Modes of Electricity Production", Elsevier, 2018, pp. 69–80.)

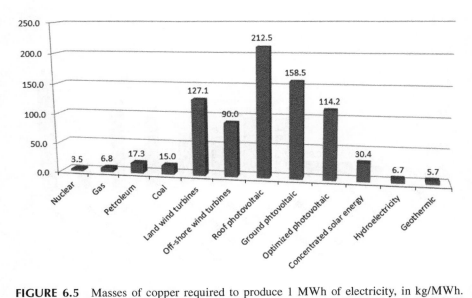

FIGURE 6.5 Masses of copper required to produce 1 MWh of electricity, in kg/MWh. (From: Olivier Vidal, *Mineral Resources and Energy*, Chapter 5 "Average Material Intensity for Various Modes of Electricity Production", Elsevier, 2018, pp. 69–80.)

mobilizes 7–8% of the world energy, and that the limits to mining extraction are not a matter of quantity but of the amount of energy. He also explains that consumption of lithium required by batteries might be multiplied by a factor of 180 between 2013 and 2035!

A study conducted by Robert I. McDonald, Joseph Fargione et al., titled "Energy Sprawl or Energy Efficiency: Climate Policy Impacts on Natural Habitat for the United States of America" [McDonald], focuses on the impact of the use of land for the development of new energy sources. Four out of the five authors of this publication are members of The Nature Conservancy, a non-profit environmental organization based in the United States since 1951. The fifth author is a university lecturer. The intensity of the use of land by the various production techniques is illustrated in Figure 6.6 and expressed in km² per terawatt-hour produced per year.

The consumption of land by wind energy is questionable as long as fields can still be cultivated in the impacted areas. It is the same for photovoltaic energy if panels are installed on roofs. We note the enormous land use resulting from the biomass, i.e. plants. The authors are concerned about the impact on forests and meadows that could be caused by an increase in energy-dedicated farming. Nuclear energy is by far the technique requiring the smallest surface area.

In my opinion the shortage of all kinds of resources will be lower if there is more energy available to pump, depollute, recycle, mine from greater depths, extract ores from the sea-bed and, why not, from space! It will often be difficult and ecosystems are likely to be impacted, but it is possible if a lot of energy is available. This leads us back to the fundamental returned-energy rate! At the moment, nuclear energy,

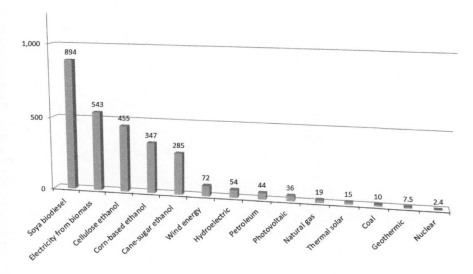

FIGURE 6.6   Surfaces impacted by various energy-production techniques, average values in km^2 per TWh per year. (From: Robert I. McDonald, Joseph Fargione, Joe Kiesecker, William M. Miller, Jimmie Powell, "Energy Sprawl or Energy Efficiency: Climate Policy Impacts on Natural Habitat for the United States of America", Plosone, August 2009, volume 4, Issue 8, [Mc Donald].)

with its considerable production potential, is the only one to feature a good EROEI and to consume a relatively small amount of materials in comparison with its production capacity. It thus represents a definite hope of an alternative to fossil energy sources in the long term, allowing rich countries' human beings to maintain their living standard.

7 Energy Transition Scenarios

Several organizations and associations have worked out energy transition scenarios for France. I have studied some of them and tried to compare them.

7.1 NEGAWATT SCENARIOS [NÉGAWATT 2011, 2017]

Among the French energy transition scenarios, Négawatt is undoubtedly the best known. It was worked out by the association of the same name. It refers to all the energy consumed in France, and not just electricity. While renewable energy sources accounted for not more than 11% of our needs in primary energy and 16% in final energy in 2018, they would almost cover them all by 2050. The implementation of this scenario would make it possible to do without both fossil and nuclear energy. The hypotheses published in 2018 [NégaWatt Hypothèses] help us to better understand how difficult such a challenge may be.

This scenario assumes that considerable efforts would be made towards renewable energy, particularly wind and photovoltaic, which would be experiencing spectacular growth.

Wind energy would have to supply 247 TWh by 2050 as opposed to 28 TWh in 2018, i.e. 9 times as much! This would involve about 20,000 land wind turbines and 4,000 off-shore turbines, while we have 7,000 land turbines and no off-shore turbines currently. The total power of the installed stock would have to be as high as 77 GW as opposed to 15 GW in 2019. The lifespan of these machines being shorter than 25 years, the current installation rate would have to be doubled at least just to maintain the 77 GW installed power capacity.

Photovoltaic installations should then supply 147 TWh each as opposed to 10 TWh as in 2018, which means that the power of the photovoltaic stock should jump from 8 to 140 GW! Given that less than an average 1 GW has been installed per year over the last 5 years and that the panel lifespan does not exceed 30 years, or even some 15 years for the connected electronic components, the installation rate in the future should reach almost 5 GW, i.e. 5 times the current rate, just to maintain a 140 GW installed power capacity! Let us note that the hypothesis adopted by the Environment and Energy Management Agency in its 2019 report [Ademe 2019] is that the solar capacity cannot grow more than by 3 GW per year while it should be doubled.

I am not sure that wind turbine and solar panel-manufacturing plants would be capable of such output if all countries were to follow suit or that the required land and skilled staff would be available.

I am not sure either, that such a development of photovoltaic energy would be very environmentally friendly given the significant environmental impacts related to the manufacturing of panels, the poor returned energy rate due to the large amount of energy consumed by the fabrication processes and, to top it all, its inability to produce energy at night when consumption is at its highest which implies the use of other systems.

Intermittence problems, i.e. no production in the evening without wind, would essentially be solved by the production and storage of methane and hydrogen – "Power to Gas". Huge investments, about which Négawatt gives very little information, would then be necessary in electricity-to-gas transforming factories, a technology which is still at an experimental stage. How and where should these factories be built, and how can gas be stored? Négawatt also counts on 18.3-TWh storage by STEP – pumping energy-transfer station – while the present potential in France is less than half of that required, and they do not make it clear where the huge water reservoirs required would be built.

But this not the main point. In spite of these huge efforts, according to Négawatt, the demand for primary energy should be reduced by 65% while the population would increase by 15%. This huge reduction would come from energy efficiency and sobriety. Efficiency means improving techniques to get the same services with lower consumption. It has gained a nearly unanimous approval without being easy to implement and would not contribute to the reduction by more than 40%. The main factor would be energy sobriety which, according to Négawatt, consists in favouring the most useful uses, "restricting the most extravagant ones and cancelling the most harmful". Interesting debates are coming to consider what is fit or unfit to do! We would have to have access to fewer goods and services, which means accepting not so rich a lifestyle.

Residential and tertiary building consumption would drop by 49% thanks to a stabilized number of inhabitants per home – fewer single people? – a development towards smaller collective housing – should the construction of individual houses be banned? – slower growth of constructions – the number of dwelling units built per year would be divided by 3 and their surface area reduced by 25% – and optimized heating systems and insulation, which I encourage.

According to Négawatt, 780,000 dwelling units would have to be renovated in order to limit the needs in heating to an average consumption of 40 kWh/m². Is it possible? The average consumption per home in France is currently close to 200 kWh per m², which is very far from 40. In 2012, the French state had set the objective of renovating 500,000 houses per year, which was seen as "a definitely unreachable goal" by the newspaper *Le Monde* on June 4th, 2014. The energy-transition related bill in favour of green growth, passed in 2015, also planned, without specifying a consumption target, 500,000 renovations per year, an objective that was not met since less than 300,000 houses are being renovated each year. The 2018 Hulot plan also planned 500,000, a far lower objective than Négawatt's 780,000. Renovating a house does not mean that its consumption will reach a low enough level. There is much to gain on a poorly insulated house, going from 300 to 150 kWh/m² per year for example, but it is very difficult with older housing to go as far down as 50.

According to CELR, *Comité de Liaison pour les Énergies Renouvelables* – renewable energy liaison committee – renamed as *Réseau pour la transition énergétique* – energy transition network – out of 300,000 housing renovations achieved in 2018, not more than 40,000 reached the "low consumption" level.

These considerations make me think that Négawatt's objective is extremely optimistic. It is a crucial point since heating accounts for about 80% of the energy consumed in buildings, which represent the primary sector for energy consumption in France, heating accounting for over a third of the final energy consumed in France. I think that the energy consumption related to heating systems will reach an average of 40 kWh/m^2 per year when energy runs out and inhabitants feel the cold.

In transport systems, the number of kilometres travelled per person each year would drop by 26%, which would run counter to the evolution we have been experiencing. In this vision, the number of journeys of over 1,500 kms (930 miles) would be reduced by half: no more domestic flights, and international flights reduced by 33%. The use of individual passenger vehicles would be reduced by half in the countryside compared with today and would be banned in large cities. Private car occupancy rate in the countryside should increase by 50% to an average of 2.4 persons per vehicle as opposed to today's 1.59. Goods transport would decrease by 17%.

Travelling less does not just mean going less on holidays. It implies fewer visits to family and friends, fewer exchanges with other people, more problems in working, buying food or construction materials etc.

Industrial energy consumption would decrease thanks to better efficiency and a reduction in the requirement for materials: –26% steel, –35% plastic, –39% cement, –41% glass. This drop implies a lower consumption of manufactured products taking place in a degrowth economy, which very few politicians wish, and is associated with more factories being likely to close.

Among other concerns, let us mention:

- A 29% drop in the consumption of hot water per head
- A 22% drop in the number of washing machine cycles
- An 18% drop in the number of dishwasher cycles
- An 18% drop in the number of tumble-dryer cycles
- A 50% drop in household freezers
- A 33% drop in the use of domestic irons
- A drop from 8 to 5 hours of lighting per day in the tertiary sector
- Disappearance of game consoles
- A 33% drop in the number of screens per household
- A 66% drop in the number of computers per household
- A 50% drop in the number of music-playing devices

7.2   THE GREENPEACE SCENARIO [GREENPEACE 2013]

For France, Greenpeace suggests a scenario that is quite similar to Négawatt's, in which the demand for primary energy by 2050 would drop by 63% and by 52% in final energy. Renewable energy sources would then meet 92% of the needs, nuclear energy would have disappeared but not fossil energies. The reduction in our needs would be due to more efficient transport systems, shorter travelling distances, housing insulation, more efficient appliances, etc.

Generally speaking, I observe that the changes suggested by Négawatt and Greenpeace would have considerable and rather unpleasant consequences in our lifestyles, and I find it hard to imagine how a vast collective awareness of environmental stakes could impose them with joy and enthusiasm. *Virage Energie*, an association closely aligned with Négawatt, suggests a 70% drop in the consumption of clothes, 50% of household cleaning products, 50% of cosmetic and toiletry products, 50% of tumble-dryers, dishwashers, freezers, audio-visual devices, 50% of refrigerator sizes, the use of collective washing machines, a reduction in acceptable household temperature, size of homes, long-distance tourism and aircraft journeys, a decrease in hotel stays etc. One may wonder whether the recommended changes are compatible with democracy, as they involve, in fact, changes in lifestyle so significant that it is possible that they may have to be imposed by force. A strong bias is likely to occur, with well-off people maintaining comfortable living conditions and the poor having to make do with harsher ones. Sooner or later, the inevitable dwindling of available fossil energy sources will certainly force human beings to consume less and the purpose of these scenarios is to prepare them for that. Yet, I blame those scenarios for giving a toned-down presentation of the huge human issues due to the drastic drop in energy consumption they require and for advocating a nuclear phase-out policy at all costs. The aim of some members of these associations is probably to show that it is possible to do without nuclear energy without enduring serious consequences. As we can neither count on fossil energy sources nor claim that renewable energies will be sufficient, the only solution left consists in claiming that a drop in consumption is not an issue. I am afraid this drop might be so difficult that human beings will carry on greedily consuming fossil energy so long as its production is easy and its benefit important.

7.3   A *BL ÉVOLUTION* STUDY ON A 1.5°C-COMPATIBLE PATH [BL]

BL évolution is a French sustainable development consultancy company. They published a study in 2019 presenting a possible path for France that would be compatible with a 1.5°C global warming limitation. The aim is to help in understanding the importance of the efforts required for the French carbon footprint to be reduced by two-thirds by 2030.

As the authors of this study have chosen the hypothesis of a 20-GW shutdown of nuclear energy by 2030, out of the 63 GW existing in 2019, and as the required reduction of fossil energy consumption cannot be compensated by an increase in renewable energy production, the resulting measures to be taken are drastic. A few examples:

- Ban on any construction of new individual houses
- 2°C reduction in the average temperature of homes, turning off heating systems that are not carbon-free between 10 p.m. and 6 a.m.

- 20% reduction of the space used per person
- Graduated taxation of electricity
- Ban on the construction of any new tertiary space
- Ban on the sale of light-goods vehicles with internal combustion-engines
- Removal of domestic flights that can be replaced by road or rail solutions of less than 4 hours
- Ban on HGVs within urban areas – 110 km/h (68 mph) speed limit on motorways
- Ban on the sale of vehicles with a fuel consumption higher than 4 litres/100 km (70.63 mpg) by 2020, 3 litres/100km (94.17 mpg) by 2023 and 2 litres/100km (141.25 mpg) in 2027
- Ban on internal combustion-engine vehicles in urban areas
- Ban on any unjustified flights outside Europe
- Ban on sales of TV sets larger than 40 inches (102 cm)
- Ban on online advertising integrated into websites
- Limitation to 1 kg brand new clothes per year and per person

The authors are lucid enough to mention that their scenario is not that realistic, that the globalization of the economy makes it impossible to comply with objectives if all countries do not trigger such an important switch and that a path compatible with a 1.5°C maximum global warming is very unlikely. These honest details contrast sharply with Négawatt's and Greenpeace's optimistic scenarios.

7.4   THE THIRD INDUSTRIAL REVOLUTION [RIFKIN]

The third industrial revolution is a theory put forward by the American economist Jeremy Rifkin. It relies on renewable energy, energy-producing buildings, energy storage in buildings, energy exchanges through smart networks and electric vehicles. In general, Jeremy Rifkin claims that society will be able to carry on consuming energy wantonly. In his book, he never quantifies the potential of these techniques to compare them to our needs. He never mentions energy efficiency which is yet unanimously recognized. Counting on wind turbines and solar panels installed on top of buildings to produce all our energy is mere utopia. Besides, Jeremy Rifkin is criticized by pro- as well as by anti-nuclearists, by growth as well as by degrowth advocates [Bellal] [Gadrey blog]. Some policy-makers like him because he is optimistic and makes people dream, but his theories are definitely unrealistic.

The third industrial revolution master plan for the Northern France region *Nord-Pas-de-Calais* [Master TRI] unveiled in October 2013 unfortunately is inspired by Rifkin's theories. I am glad that my region has considered the problem of energy seriously, but I do not understand why such an American utopian was selected rather than an engineer understanding these problems, which are first and foremost technical and scientific. The master plan has fortunately introduced such concepts as energy efficiency and circular economy, i.e. recycling, which are missing in Rifkin's book about the third industrial revolution. The energy-sobriety subject failed to win unanimous support because defining what is related to energy wastage is not an easy task and sobriety probably implies degrowth. It is therefore missing in the plan predicting a 60% drop in energy consumption while maintaining services, which means relying on energy efficiency only. It seems to be more ambitious as compared to other scenarios, all the more so as a strong rise in the GDP (+47%), i.e. of human activity, is predicted at the same time. To my knowledge, this scenario is the only one to claim that a drop in the consumption of energy can be compatible with a rising GDP. The idea is that since renewable energy is free, money can be spent for purposes other than energy and will therefore fuel the economy. I doubt that renewable energy will ever be really free. Indeed, petroleum, coal and gas, as well as sun and wind have always been available for free by nature but have never been so for consumers. If it was the case, a decrease in consumption would certainly not be stimulated. I think that the rising of GDP necessarily means an increase in goods and services exchanges, hence in human activity and in the energy needed. This scenario is designed to reach the 100%-renewable energy level by 2050, but there is no technical detail mentioning by what miracle. Actually, neither any renewable energy production potential nor energy-saving sector by sector is quantified in this master plan. The benefit of this operation was to promote the awareness of the importance of the energy issue through extensive communication exchanges. It fosters energy-related research and teaching activities and promotes some positive actions about the example of energy efficiency or biogas. Six years after its launch, it is undoubtedly too early to draw a first assessment of this operation. Anyway, energy consumption in the North of France slightly increased between 2014 and 2017 by 1.3%, mainly thanks to the residential sector.

7.5 ADEME'S SCENARIOS [ADEME 2013]

In 2013, ADEME – the French environment and energy management agency – published scenarios for France for the years 2030 and 2050 in a study titled *Contribution de l'ADEME à l'élaboration de visions énergétiques 2030–2050. Synthèse avec évaluation macroéconomique* – ADEME's contribution to the development of 2030–2050 energy visions. A synthesis and a macroeconomic evaluation. With the aim to reduce greenhouse gas emissions by three-quarters by 2050, ADEME recommends a 47% drop in final energy, in its "median" scenario. Renewable energy would supply 55% of total needs, the rest being covered by oil, gas and nuclear energy, which means these sources would play a significant part. Table 7.1 is an extract from the report. It gives ranges of primary energy sources as in 2050, according to three scenarios granting a different place to nuclear energy. It shows that the major primary energy sources would be, in descending order: nuclear energy, wood – the combustion of which is not free from any pollution or impact on health – wind energy, natural gas – fossil – and biogas. As nuclear energy features a relatively low yield, it is certainly granted excessive importance as a primary energy source but would still keep an important role.

In 2017, ADEME published an update of these studies [Ademe 2017] with three scenarios. None of them considers the ruling out of fossil or nuclear energy which

TABLE 7.1

2050 Primary Energy Sources, in TWh

		Minimum	Maximum
Renewables	Biosourced solid fuels	199	199
	Wind	106	162
	Biogas	102	102
	Geothermy	59	70
	Hydroelectricity	50	67
	Photovoltaic	42	70
	Material (except biofuel wood)	65	65
	Air calories	28	28
	Thermal solar	21	21
	Waste	15	15
	Ocean energy	6	45
	Total renewables	**693**	**844**
Nuclear and	Nuclear	251	670
Fossil	Natural gas	138	138
	Petroleum	69	69
	Coal	47	47
	Waste	16	16
	Total nuclear and fossil	**521**	**940**

ADEME scenarios [ADEME 2013].

would still account for at least 31% of final energy and renewable energy for 46 to 69% depending on the part played by nuclear energy.

In the three cases, a 45% drop of consumption is necessary. It would result, for example, in renovating 750,000 homes per year from 2030, building fewer new homes and reducing their surface area, developing shared housing, adopting more sober behaviours, using more efficient appliances, carpooling and car-sharing, tele-working, using more efficient and lighter electric or gas-fuelled vehicles, a 24% reduction of our mobility, the development of railways and waterways for the transport of goods, a drop in meat consumption, optimized industrial activities, etc. What an ambitious programme!

Among the three scenarios, the one requiring the least nuclear and fossil energies implies the implementation of large energy-storage infrastructures (by STEP and power-to-gas) which are known to be complex.

As ADEME does not envisage any increase in nuclear-produced electricity, natural gas would have an important role to play. As a consequence, greenhouse gas emissions would be reduced by 72% maximum, which means that the "factor of four" would not be fully reached.

7.6 L'AGENCE NATIONALE POUR LA COORDINATION DE LA RECHERCHE POUR L'ÉNERGIE [ANCRE] (FRENCH ENERGY RESEARCH NATIONAL COORDINATION AGENCY)

ANCRE coordinates French public research organizations. In 2013, it published three scenarios aiming at reducing CO_2 emissions by three-quarters: while renewable energy sources would be largely developed and without ruling out nuclear energy, final energy consumption would go from 27 to 41% thanks to steady efforts made towards energy efficiency. ANCRE highlights the fact that the factor of four will only be reached thanks to important efforts and the use of disruptive technology processes such as CO_2 storage, electricity storage, nuclear cogeneration, etc.

7.7 NÉGATEP'S SCENARIOS [NÉGATEP]

Négatep's scenarios were written by members of the French association *Sauvons le Climat*, and by Claude Acket and Pierre Bacher, in particular. Their objective is to fight against global warming through energy savings that would result from efficiency and sobriety, as well as through the partial replacement of fossil fuels by nuclear and renewable energy sources. Several versions of this work have been released since 2007, the latest dating from 2017. Its forecast for 2050 is a reduction by three-quarters of the consumption of fossil energy sources in spite of a drop of only about 20% of final energy consumption with respect to that of 2015. Fossil energy sources would be largely replaced by renewable ones (+45% electric renewable sources, +135% thermal renewable ones) and by nuclear energy (+57%). The production of electricity would increase by 55%. Electric vehicles and heat-pump systems would be widely developed. As a result, this scenario recommends a considerable increase in the role of electricity as it would be produced without any CO_2 emissions, particularly thanks to nuclear power stations. This would imply the construction of new and more powerful nuclear reactors, evolutionary power reactors (EPR), to make up for the gradual shutdown of the reactors reaching their end-of-life. Building a nuclear reactor is certainly a complex operation considering the problems experienced with the construction of Flamanville EPR. But France was able to build in no more than 26 years the 58 reactors that were still operational in 2019. It must thus be possible to build others. Flamanville EPR was a newly designed plant, the very first evolutionary power reactor ever produced. The technology it uses is different from the one previous reactors relied on. We may hope that the construction of the next EPRs will not face any more teething problems and be eventually produced in series as was the case with previous reactors built in the years 1970–1980. It was particularly pretentious to announce that this new reactor would be built in less than 5 years while it took 8 to 13 years to connect the previous newly designed French reactors to the grid [Foos]. By the way, two EPRs are operational in Taishan, China. One opened in 2018 and the other in 2019. According to Négatep, a 100-GW nuclear-installed power capacity would be required in France, as opposed to 63 GW in 2019. It could be obtained thanks to 64 EPRs, but, considering that the lifespan of a reactor is 60 years, we would have to be able to open an average of one reactor per year.

This pace seems to be quite conceivable since France was able to start up an average of four reactors per year during the 1980s. However, considering the shutdown of current reactors which are reaching the end of their lifespans and the time required for studies and construction processes, a 100-GW installed power capacity in France by 2050 seems extremely unlikely to me.

Of course, Négatep's scenario makes anti-nuclearists red with anger as they accuse the *Sauvons le Climat* association of preserving nuclear energy. I have the impression that the members of this association have an extensive knowledge of the complexity of the problem represented by the production of electricity, particularly concerning the network balance. They also know nuclear energy well and consider that this energy is a valuable asset for the future. Therefore, they logically recommend increasing its role along with renewable ones in order to rule out fossil sources.

These scenarios, as well as others, were studied during the French national debate about energy transition, organised in 2012 and 2013 by the Environment, Sustainable Development and Energy Minister. The conclusions gave rise to four trajectories including drops of final energy from 17 to 50% by 2050. The objective approved in 2015 was a 50% reduction by 2050. I am not sure that the policy makers who voted for this objective are all aware of the links between energy and the economy. This objective was included in the Energy Multi-Year Programme and in the 2019 French Energy-Climate law.

We can observe that no French scenario states that fossil and nuclear energy sources can be replaced by renewable ones without a large reduction in consumption.

Considering these various scenarios regarding the whole French energy system, the potential production of renewable energy sources with the use of current technologies accounts for less than half the French energy consumption. All scenarios recommend an important reduction of energy consumption in spite of an increasing population. All scenarios mostly rely on energy efficiency, the importance of which is crucial.

The following two scenarios only concern electricity in France.

7.8   ADEME'S STUDY: *A 100% RENEWABLE ELECTRIC MIX* [ADEME 2015] [ADEME 2018]

In spring 2015, journalists revealed a report from ADEME that was said to be explosive and the publishing of which was supposed to have been stopped by lobbies because it was demonstrating the possibility of doing without nuclear and fossil energy sources and replacing them by renewable ones. One may wonder why ADEME, which nobody claims to be in the pay of the lobbies, would have ordered such a study just to conceal it afterwards. The completed report was eventually released in its official version in autumn 2015 [Ademe 2015]. Some journalists and politicians hastily concluded that renewable energy sources could easily replace fossil and nuclear ones. A new version, including economic aspects in particular, was published at the end of 2018 [Ademe 2018].

If there is one thing that we should remember about this study (which is not a transition scenario) it is that it only concerns electricity which accounts for less than a quarter of the French energy. It does not consider the use of wood or biogas to produce electricity, which means that these sources would then be less available to supply heating systems. It does not wonder about the way to replace fuel-oil or gas building heating systems – possibly by electric ones – or the fact that most transport systems are petroleum-fuelled. Actually, this was not the aim of this work, which was "of a prospective and exploratory nature".

This study relies on a large development of solar energy and a very large development of wind energy. As their production varies according to meteorological conditions, the authors wondered about energy storage and rotor-furling systems to be implemented, hence producing a very complex work which I don't personally mean to question, though others did. However, I think that the enthusiasm aroused by this study can be tempered as its "reference" scenario considers:

- A reduction in electricity net consumption down to 422 TWh per year as opposed to the 2018 440 TWh, this being reached in spite of 10 million electric vehicles – out of the French 40 million vehicles. The consumption of these 10 million vehicles accounting for at least 30 TWh per year, there would be less than 392 TWh left for current uses, which means an 11% reduction compared to the current 440-TWh consumption. Residential consumption would decrease by 29.5%, and industrial consumption by 23.5%. As the population will increase in the future, some polluting fuel-oil or gas systems would be replaced by electric ones which makes the 11% consumption drop rather optimistic. French consumption has actually been quite steady since 2018: it has not decreased or just slightly.
- Times when electricity would have to be imported from foreign countries, which would not necessarily be supplied by renewable sources: 35 TWh from non-renewable sources. And ADEME even writes that "most imports exploit the fossil flexibility of our neighbours' electric systems"!
- Battery storage with a very poor environmental balance. Several million tons of batteries would be required, with a limited lifespan.
- An increased number of STEPs – artificial lakes and dams – with no mention of where new huge reservoirs would be built. Let us keep in mind the strong opposition to the Sivens dam.
- Important "power-to-gas" storage, a technique transforming electricity into gas, hydrogen or methane, and then back into electricity. This method is certainly promising but still in its infancy. Relying largely on it is therefore rather ambitious. In the study, there is little information about the infrastructures that will have to be built or the possible constraints.
- A huge development of wind energy with an annual 303-TWh production, though it does not exceed the 200 TWh in ADEME's 2017 "all energy sources" study, a gap that I find surprising. As wind energy production in France was 28 TWh in 2018, at least ten times as many wind turbines would be necessary.

- An optimistic 31% load factor for land-based wind energy load factor, while it is 21% on average in France nowadays and is obtained thanks to new-generation wind turbines (the load factor is the ratio between the actual average power and the installed power capacity; it takes the actual wind into account).
- A 96-GW installed power capacity, as opposed to 15 in 2018. Given that about 1.5 GW have been installed per year in France in recent years and that the lifespan of a wind turbine is probably less than 25 years, the installation pace should thus be tripled in order to get 3 times as much manufacturing capacity, skilled staff, cranes, etc.
- Important consumption deferments – 60 TWh – for factories, home heating, hot water production or domestic appliance usage. Depending on the strength of wind and sunlight, their working would have to be deferred in times when production is inadequate. So, ADEME considers that industrial consumption is 55% flexible, domestic consumption 56%, heating 75%, electric vehicles charging 80%. I consider this aspect as fundamental. If we agree to consume electricity only when the wind is blowing, wind energy is obviously the most pertinent! I have difficulty imagining that the running of factories and heating systems can be deferred that much. Will electric vehicle users agree to wait to recharge at the risk of having an insufficiently charged battery when leaving? Will it be possible for industrialists to defer their production processes? In any case, it is a tendency towards a minimum effort principle since workers' schedules would sometimes have to be put back or forward, people would have to avoid heating their homes when it is cold or cooking when they are hungry, etc. An insufficiently refined supply-on-demand model (hour by hour). The authors themselves point out that the management of the electric grid's stability is not dealt with in the study. Indeed, a permanent adjustment of the powers consumed and produced requires very complex control loops which are currently facilitated by the huge inertia of large alternator spinning masses [Sapy]. Nobody currently knows whether a network being supplied via the necessary electronics – placed in between solar panels, wind turbines, batteries and electric transmission lines – would be able to supply the necessary electricity demands, for example when a TGV starts. According to specialists, "mastering the security of such a system" requires new solutions, the technical operation and scaling of which remain to be validated [Systèmes]. ADEME actually mentions that "more in-depth analyses would be required of this aspect of the electrical system".

The major conclusion I draw from this report is that it would be very difficult to have a 100% renewable electric mix in France.

Engineers and physicists Dominique Grand, Christian Lebrun and Roland Vidil produced an in-depth analysis of this study. In an article published in *La Revue de l'énergie* [Grand] in May 2016, they conclude that "the total installed power capacity required to achieve the mix would represent more than twice the current value", that "the contribution of gas produced through methanization is not sufficient to make up for the lack in production", that "fossil fuels have to be burnt" and that "the 100% renewable scenario would result in greenhouse gas emissions in an approximately equal proportion compared with the current mix".

Dominique Finon, a researcher in economics and energy specialist, qualifies ADEME's hypotheses on the improvement of energy efficiency as "very optimistic", and their economic hypotheses as "heroic". He observes that the furling power is at least 60 GW in the scenario while it was just 2 GW in France in 2018 and that RTE estimates a maximum 9 GW can be reached by 2030. He also observes that interconnection capacities – i.e. electric interconnections through borders – would have to be tripled [Finon SPS].

In December 2018, the *Académie des Technologies*, a French scientific academy whose aim is to enlighten society about the best use of technologies, asserted that "the conclusions of the ADEME study must be regarded very cautiously" and "should in no case serve as a basis for public political decisions" [Académie].

Sylvain Lassonde's conclusion in his doctoral thesis on the theme of "potentials and meteorological and climate limits of the smoothing of renewable energies": "we have also shown that the events dimensioning the important volumes of stored energy correspond to periods which have not been studied by others, such as ADEME", and thinks that this organization did not consider climatic variations over a long enough period [Lassonde].

My impression is that some people absolutely wanted to produce an undeniable proof of the feasibility of a nuclear phase-out without using fossil fuels and that hypotheses were chosen accordingly in order to get to the desired conclusions. It is clear that ADEME is not directed by the nuclear lobby.

Irrespective of intermittence and storage problems, ADEME's study asserts that the theoretical maximum potential renewable energy is 1,268 TWh in France, while declaring that "nothing can guarantee harmony between production and demand at all times". Therefore, this figure does not mean that all this energy can be made available, as the inevitable loss due to transmission and storage, and particularly what is not possible to store, has to be subtracted. Although this figure may seem quite optimistic compared to the previous scenarios, it remains largely inferior to the French consumption of energy – almost 1,800 TWh final energy and more than 3,000 TWh primary energy – and just confirms the previous conclusions: **our energy consumption would have to be reduced considerably to rule out fossil and nuclear energy sources.**

7.9   RTE SCENARIOS: 50% NUCLEAR [RTE BP 2017]

The 2015 energy transition law towards green growth specified that the nuclear part in the production of electricity must be reduced to 50% by 2025. Therefore, the French public service *Réseau de Transport de l'Electricité* (RTE – electricity transmission network) published, in November 2017, several scenarios that help understand how challenging the objective may be. As the scenario named "Ohm" showed that there should have been an increase in gas-produced electricity, hence in CO_2

emissions, the objective was put off to 2035. The scenarios named "Ampère", "Volt", "Hertz" and "Watt" are related to this objective. They mainly examine replacing part of the nuclear pool by wind turbines and solar panels as shown in Table 7.2 giving a comparison to 2016, the reference year. Electricity being difficult to store, production must constantly be adapted to demand thanks to adjustable controllable methods (nuclear, fossil, hydraulic, biomass). This requires increasing their number. So, RTE considers 10% of wind energy installed power capacity can be counted on most of the time, which roughly means that ten wind turbines have to be installed to perhaps get at least the power of a single one.

The most commented on of the scenarios is *Ampère*. It plans for electricity to be produced 46% by nuclear, 50% by renewable and 4% by fossil energy sources. Let us analyse how:

- Electricity production would increase by 20% in spite of stagnating consumption. Actually, the objective is 50% of the production and not 50% of the consumption from nuclear. By increasing exports, nuclear production would still account for 61% of the French consumption but less than 50% of the production. Some people see in this view the influence of the nuclear lobby who would have found there a means to shut down as few reactors as possible. But with wind and solar production irregularity requiring an increase in the number of installations in order to ensure a minimum energy when wind or sunlight are low, there would be times when it would be in excess and should be exported. Thereby, a 213-TWh increase in renewable production would only result in a possible 90-TWh decrease in nuclear production.
- The total installed power capacity would increase by 62%, from 129 to 209 GW. Production means would then have to be increased considerably for the same consumption. New wind turbines and solar panels would add to other production means but not replace them. The installation pace of wind turbines would have to be tripled and that of photovoltaic panels doubled. RTE mentions that "this trajectory is ambitious and requires a dimension change as compared to the current situation".
- Annual electricity consumption would stagnate in spite of a growing population, a 2% economic growth and over 15 million electric vehicles. The major argument put forward is an improved energy efficiency. Yet, French consumption has been stagnating since 2008 and has not decreased while economic growth has been less than 2%. RTE considers that 700,000 homes could be renovated per year for better insulation. We have seen how ambitious this objective can be.
- Peak consumption should decrease as wind and solar production would not necessarily be there at the right time. RTE points out that as very low temperature episodes resulting in consumption peaks often occur when wind production is low, they could only be covered thanks to imports. Despite that, RTE explains that "supply and demand balance during high consumption situations necessarily relies on a contribution of wind energy", which

TABLE 7.2
Summary of RTE's Scenarios Leading to 50% Nuclear Energy by 2035 [RTE BP 2017]

	In 2016	Amp 2035	Volt 2035	Hertz 2035	Watt 2035
Production in TWh	531	630	617	536	440
Gross consumption in TWh	483	480	442	480	410
% of nuclear consumption	79.5	61.3	78.3	52.5	11.7
% of nuclear production	72.3	46.7	56.0	47.0	11.0
% of renewable production	19.0	50.0	40.0	45.0	70.0
% of fossil production	9.0	4.0	4.0	8.0	18.0
Nuclear power in gw	63.1	48.5	55.0	39.0	8.0
Nuclear production in Twh	384.0	294.0	346.0	252.0	48.0
Land wind-power in GW	11.7	52.0	40.0	40.0	52.0
Land wind production in TWh	20.7	115.0	88.0	88.0	115.0
Ocean wind-power in GW	0.0	15.0	10.0	10.0	15.0
Ocean wind production in TWh	0.0	47.0	29.0	29.0	47.0
Solar power in GW	6.8	48.0	36.0	36.0	48.0
Solar production in TWh	8.3	58.0	43.0	43.0	58.0
% of non-controllable production	5.5	34.9	25.9	29.9	50.0
Thermal power in GW	20.4	13.2	10.0	23.2	34.4
Thermal production in TWh	44.5	27.6	23.7	45.7	78.8
Non-controllable power in GW	18.0	115.0	86.0	86.0	115.0
Controllable power in GW	111.0	94.0	95.0	93.0	77.0
Total installed power in GW	129.0	209.0	181.0	179.0	192.0
CO_2 emissions in Mt	22.0	12.0	9.0	19.0	32.0

is dependent on weather conditions. As a consequence, the probability of failure may be up to 30% for installed power capacities higher than 94 GW and up to 60% for consumption higher than 101 GW. But the 2018 peak was 97 GW and France's highest peak ever was 102 GW in 2012. RTE actually confirms that "power demands higher than 100 GW could still occur by 2035, which questions the level ensured" as "the French electricity system is no longer in a position to cope with a cold spell such as in February 2012 without calling upon exceptional levers or even selective power cuts". RTE also writes that "in 2035, out of the 1,000 simulated cases, 44% represent at least a one-hour failure and 5% a more than 10-hour failure". In plain language, RTE's warning is that there will be power cuts!

The Volt scenario is the one using the least gas, thereby leading to a higher decrease in CO_2 emissions. But it supposes an 8% drop in the annual electricity consumption and, most importantly, it maintains the part played by nuclear energy at a level higher than 56%. The risk of failure is lower.

The Hertz scenario plans lower nuclear production but higher gas production, hence resulting in CO_2 emissions close to current ones and a higher risk of failure.

The Watt scenario leads to only 11% nuclear, but it supposes an important drop in consumption (15%) and the doubling of fossil production, hence a significant increase in CO_2 emissions (+45%). It requires the most important demand-side management, which does not guard against the very high 85% risk of failure (!) for consumption peaks of only 89 GW.

The Hertz and Watt scenarios, which are the ones leading to the highest reduction of nuclear energy, were abandoned as their CO_2 emissions were the highest.

To sum up, replacing part of nuclear or fossils power stations by wind and solar solutions would require more electrical load management operations/deferments and sometimes power cuts, a considerable increase in the total installed power capacity and transmission lines, a reduction of the annual consumption and peaks and the opportunity for our neighbours to purchase electricity from us when we produce too much as well as for them to sell some to us when needed. The lower the part played by nuclear energy, the higher the CO_2 emissions and the higher the risk of power cuts.

The following scenarios concern the world's total energy consumption (not only electricity).

7.10 THE WIND WATER SUN SCENARIO [WWS] BY STANFORD UNIVERSITY

The Wind Water Sun project from Stanford University (also named "The Solutions Project") strives to supply the planet's total energy by electrifying all uses from wind, water and sun without reducing comfort! There is no shortage of criticisms! Philippe Bihouix writes that the project leader,

> Mark Jacobson, has obviously never walked into a factory and does not know that the manufacturing and installation of a beautiful and clean wind turbine requires the use

of steel, cement, polyurethane resins, rare earth and copper, ships and cranes, amongst other things.

[Bihouix low tech]

And 3.8 million 5-MW wind turbines and 89,000 300-MW solar power stations would be required, hence the installation of a 19,000-GW wind turbine power capacity in fifteen years' time (thirty times the current maximum 40-GW per year) and the inauguration of fifteen solar power stations every day.

[Bihouix mythe]

Reviewing the potentials of renewable energies of such a country as France, as did ADEME, is already a very difficult exercise requiring the making of a comprehensive list of the potential production sites but also taking into account meteorological statistics, potential storage sites, constraints on electric networks, etc. Therefore, I doubt whether this work can be achieved on a global scale.

As for France, too few details are given to be able to get a good understanding as to what miracle would make it possible to do what French studies claim they cannot do. The production potentials used are higher than those from all other French scenarios. Solar and wind electricity intermittence and storage issues seem significantly underestimated. ADEME hardly ends up with 422 TWh of renewable electricity, i.e. 24% of our current energy consumption, while supposing important storage systems [ADEME 2015] while this study claims to supply our energy needs almost without any storage.

Concerning the United States, the scientific review, Proceedings of the National Academy of Sciences of the United States of America, published, in 2017, a "counter-article" to Mark Jacobson's which was signed by 21 specialists with the aim of denouncing the inconsistencies of this project [Clack]; this "counter-article" notes important shortcomings in the analysis, invalid modelling tools in particular, errors and hardly plausible hypotheses. "Energy problems are complex". Mark's simple solution attracts many of those who do not have the necessary tools to comprehend this complexity", says Jane Long, a former Lawrence Livermore National Laboratory (California) associate director. Stephen Chu, Physics Nobel prize winner in 1997 and Barack Obama's Secretary of Energy between 2009 and 2013, declared in 2019 that

reaching 100% renewable energy in so short a timeframe seems to be very difficult. Some of my colleagues from Stanford University have been claiming for twenty years that 100% renewable energy is achievable … within twenty years! This is probably not what is going to happen.

[CHU]

7.11   IPCC SCENARIOS

The IPCC examined many scenarios aiming at stabilizing global warming. In 2018, they published a report concerning a 1.5°C limitation for global warming [IPCC 2018]. It presents four typical trajectories. The world's demand in energy by 2050 varies from –32% to +44%; oil consumption falls by at least one-third, coal is hardly used, the share of renewable energy in electricity production goes up to at least 63%

(as opposed to about 25% in 2019), nuclear electricity production is multiplied by 2 to 6, renewable energy production is multiplied by about 10. Only a scenario planning a 32% drop in the world's energy consumption does not rely on tricky CO_2 underground storage technologies. François Marie Bréon, an IPCC member and climatologist, writes the following comment: "one may be doubtful about the possibility to multiply by two to six the amount of renewable energy produced per year by 2030, or to consider a 60 to 40% rise of nuclear energy by then" [Breton SPS]. Besides, the IPCC's report mentions that swift and deep transitions in the fields of energy, land, towns and infrastructure, as well as industrial systems, would be required and that these transitions would be unprecedented in terms of scale.

Concerning nuclear energy, while some of the scenarios mentioned by the IPCC assert that it is possible to do without it thanks to sobriety, renewable energy development and tricky CO_2 storage techniques, the four typical scenarios put forward by the IPCC largely rely on it. Resorting to nuclear energy appears to be all the more necessary as energy consumption increases. It is indispensable in all IPCC scenarios if CO_2 is not stored underground (Table 7.3).

7.12   GROUP GISOC'S EFFICIENCY N SCENARIO [EFFICIENCY N]

The Global Initiative to Save Our Climate (GISOC) group is composed of about 20 energy-climate specialists from 6 countries. About half of them are French and members or sympathisers of the *Sauvons le Climat* association who promote the French *Négatep* scenario. They observed that nuclear supporters are not greatly involved in the writing of IPCC scenarios and decided to show that nuclear energy can largely contribute to limiting global warming. Its 1.5°C limit requires resorting extensively

---

TABLE 7.3

IPCC Model Scenarios Leading to a Reduction of Global Warming down to 1.5°C

Scenario	P1	P2	P3	P4
Final energy demand in 2050	−32%	2%	21%	44%
Greenhouse gas emissions in 2050	−82%	−89%	−78%	−80%
Coal	−97%	−77%	−73%	−97%
Petroleum	−87%	−50%	−81%	−32%
Gas	−74%	−53%	+21%	−48%
Nuclear energy	+150%	+98%	+501%	+468%
Percentage of renewable energy in electricity production	77%	81%	63%	70%
Biomass	−16%	+49%	+121%	+418%
Non biomass-based renewable energies	+833%	+1327%	+878%	+1137%
Cumulated CO_2 storage until 2100, in billion tons	0	348	687	1218

Percentages concern the year 2050, rises or falls (+ −) refer to the year 2010 [IPCC 2018].

---

to CO_2 storage, a very uncertain technology; their Efficiency N scenario promotes the same objective but reduces this dependence by two-thirds while increasing the amount of energy available to humans. It would mean replacing the production of heat from fossil gas and the use of oil by electricity, 44% of which would be nuclear-produced by 2060 (by generation-4 fast-neutron reactors in particular), 25% from biomass, 25% from wind and solar systems and 12% from hydroelectric installations. Renewable energy production would then have to be increased considerably, but so would nuclear energy, the world's installed power capacity of which would have to reach about 6,000 GW, as opposed to less than 400 GW in 2019. To do so, nearly 4,000 reactors would be required around the world together with the capacity to open at least a hundred of them every year from 2030 on. France actually started up four reactors per year in the 1980s, and other countries are able to master nuclear systems under good safety conditions. But this ambitious scenario does not explain where all these reactors should be installed. Nuclear energy supporter as I am, I would rather see some countries refrain from developing this kind of energy and I find it hard to imagine such a growth.

8 Energy Efficiency and Sobriety

8.1 ENERGY EFFICIENCY AND PHYSICAL LIMITS

To reduce needs in energy, the "efficiency" lever wins unanimous support since it means consuming less for an equal service thanks to technology. The best example is certainly home insulation. Potential gains of efficiency seem to be difficult to evaluate accurately due to so numerous and varied energy-hungry technologies and applications. However, one should keep in mind that there are physical limits to efficiency.

The laws of physics imply energy conservation. Let us not forget that energy can only be transformed but not created. Some actions are impossible without a certain amount of energy. Here are a few examples:

- To lift a mass "M" (in kg) to a height "h" (in metres), the amount of energy "E" (in joules) required is calculated according to the relation $E = Mgh$ ("g" being the acceleration due to gravity, equal to 9.8 m/s^2 on Earth). Thereby, an elevator which has to lift a 1,000-kg load to a height of 50 m requires 490,000 joules, i.e. 136 Wh (watt-hours), if the system is perfectly loss-free (1Wh = 3.600 J).
- To move a mass "M" (in kg) at a velocity "v" (in metres per second), the energy required is $E = mv^2/2$. Therefore, to bring a 1,000-kg vehicle to a speed of 27.77 m/s (100 km/h/62.14 mph), the energy required is 385,600 joules, i.e. 107 Wh, which corresponds to approximately 0.01 litre (0.0022 imp. gal) of petrol.
- To raise the temperature of a mass "M" (in kg) with a specific heat capacity "c" (constant related to the material) to a temperature θ (in degrees Celsius), the energy required is $E = Mc\theta$. Thereby, to boil 2 litres of water from 20°C, the energy required is 669.600 joules (for water, c = 4.185 J/kg·K), i.e. 186 Wh.

No technological advance will change the results of these calculations. Actually, the amounts of energy required are significantly higher due to inevitable losses, which energy efficiency attempts to minimize. For example, to boil water, it is easy to put a lid onto the saucepan in order to minimize heat exchanges between the inside and the outside. But it is physically impossible to go below the previously mentioned thresholds.

Energy efficiency can also consist in trying to reuse stored energy. For example, when an elevator goes down, the electric motor can send energy back to the network.

When decelerating, hybrid vehicles send energy back to batteries. But, there again, an inevitable loss will occur.

To maintain a mass at a constant velocity in vacuum it is not necessary to supply energy. But in the case of a vehicle running on the Earth, air, tyre and mechanical friction are inevitable. In this case, energy efficiency consists in minimizing air friction thanks to an optimized aerodynamic design. But "optimized" will never mean "perfect".

To maintain a perfectly insulated building at a constant temperature, no energy is needed. But even very high-performance insulating materials are never perfect, so that a certain amount of energy is always required, however small it may be, to compensate for heat exchanges between the building and outside. It is actually quite easy to gain a lot of energy by fitting lofts with insulating material or replacing single- by double-glazed windows. But the more you progress the harder it is to advance. In any case, there are necessarily remaining losses which, in cold weather conditions, have to be compensated for by some solar supply, heat released by appliances of inhabitants (coming from the energy they consume), or by a heating system.

The amount of light provided by a lamp is measured in lumens. Traditional incandescent bulbs, the efficiency of which was not over 15 lumens per watt (lm/W), are now prohibited and replaced by compact fluorescent or LED ones with an efficiency that can reach 150 lm/W, i.e. ten times as much. The considerable difference is obtained thanks to a technological leap forward, but the potential saving is not huge. It has been estimated at about 8 TWh [Convention ampoules], which accounts for less than 0.5% of French energy consumption. In fact, lighting accounts for little more than 15% of electricity consumption, which represents less than a quarter of energy consumption. Besides, office, shop, warehouse and road lighting systems have not been incandescent for a long time. In the future, technology will not be able to keep progressing as there is a 200 lm/W physical limit over which white light cannot be supplied, and an absolute 683 lm/W limit whatever the visible spectral range. In addition, the lower consumption of these bulbs physically results in a lower release of heat, part of the energy saved being thereby annihilated by an extra need in heating.

Many industrial processes are naturally energy-greedy, particularly because materials need to be heated. I am not sure that producing cement, steel or glass will ever be possible without heat. Rather than letting it go to waste, it should be saved, for example to heat buildings located close to factories. But these energy efficiency solutions require complex installations and suppose that heat is needed in the nearby area.

Industrialists are currently encouraged to optimise their energy consumption. In many factories, old pieces of equipment are replaced by more efficient ones (boilers, lamps, motors), variable speed drives are installed, some appliances are turned off at night, heat reclaiming systems are developed etc. Potential gains are very varied from one firm to another and depend on the starting levels. A small number of them, which start from a very low point, may expect some 50% gains, but doing better will be very difficult.

Significant advances in energy efficiency have been achieved following the 1974 and 1979 oil crises. As a consequence, the average consumption of vehicles has measurably dropped in 40 years thanks to more efficient engines. However, today the consumption of vehicles hardly decreases any more. We seem to have reached a limit. We might have to do with smaller, less powerful, lighter cars, therefore more sparsely fitted but also probably less safe, in order to continue to gain in efficiency. For an equal service, we would then relate efficiency to sobriety. Likewise, building insulation, yet still inadequate, has significantly been improving since the 1970s. Energy efficiency is not a brand-new concept. For example, concerning lighting systems, we started minimizing consumption long before the use of LEDs. Low-pressure sodium vapour lamps, with an efficiency of almost 200 lm/W, have been used for a long time when possible. Another example: if we try to minimize the loss in a 110- kW industrial electric motor which has a 93.3% output ratio, the potential gain would account for less than 7% of the consumed energy. The easiest gains have thus already been achieved or are underway, and improvements will reach limits.

Moreover, gains in energy efficiency can be mitigated, if not cancelled out, by a rebound effect: "Energy gains obtained through the evolution of computer and television screens have been cancelled out due to the simultaneous increase of screen sizes" [Jouanno]. The increase in population and economic activity has contributed to the recent years' rise in road-vehicle fuel consumption, although consumption per vehicle has been considerably reduced. Likewise, while it is definitely a good thing that newly built buildings are qualified as "low-consumption", we have to keep in mind that each new building accounts for an extra consumption, at least when it is being built.

A lower consumption often requires an investment in more complex technologies requiring more materials, more work and more energy. Housing insulation is a good example of this: while it is sometimes possible to financially write off the required insulation works, they require extra material to be manufactured and transported but also additional labour. **It is thus more difficult** (and, clearly speaking, more expensive) **to have somewhere to live in a world where energy is scarce than in a world where energy is abundant and where we used to afford a plain building without worrying about consumption.** Many people find it difficult to find somewhere to live to start with, and the growing scarcity of energy will not help. A study published by the *Commissariat Général au Développment Durable* (sustainable development high commission) estimates the extra construction cost of a home complying with the 2012 thermal regulations (RT 2012) is 9% when collective and 14% when individual as compared to the previous regulations (RT 2005) [CGDD 135]. Some construction companies even talk about a 20% extra cost. Extra costs are even expected to increase with the new 2020 regulations.

Electric motors are another example, which I know well. To decrease their energy loss, manufacturers have to make them more voluminous, thus heavier and consuming more raw materials, or use materials the manufacturing of which is more complex and energy-hungry. Solutions are often ecologically and financially positive but make technologies more complicated.

Hybrid vehicles combine petrol-fuelled and electric motors. When running downhill or decelerating, the electric motor turns into a generator and recharges batteries which are called upon later on to reduce fuel consumption. It is a clever system, but it is undeniably more complicated and consumes more materials and electronic components than standard vehicles.

Compact fluorescent and LED lightbulbs consume less energy than incandescent ones, but they require electronic components (typically located in the cap). They are thus more complex to manufacture and use more raw materials.

Generally speaking, digital technologies can help us optimize our various consumptions using occupancy detectors, electronic thermostats, smart electric meters, measuring devices and electronic speed controllers, for example. But, as a result, our society is gradually becoming more and more dependent on electronics and energy-hungry data-centres, getting more and more complex and perhaps more and more fragile. One may sometimes want to make people dream by letting them believe that intelligence can replace energy. Smart systems can help to better manage energy but cannot create any!

The above examples are applicable to many fundamental fields of human life: **with less energy it will be more complex to get food, to move around, to be accommodated and to benefit from healthcare.**

8.2   SOLAR VEHICLES

An old dream is to fuel vehicles with solar energy. Is it possible?

The running of a vehicle requires overcoming various forms of friction, particularly air resistance, which is unavoidable on Earth. The necessary power to overcome them depends on the shape of the front part of the vehicle, its aerodynamic design and its speed. For a small car, a power of about 8,000 W at a speed of about 100 km/h (62 mph) is required to make up for just air resistance.

[*Hard-working people can check that $P = 0.5 \times \rho \times SCx \times v^3$ gives about 8,000 W with $\rho = 1.2$ (air density), $SCx = 0.6$ (coefficient for a standard car depending on its front surface and aerodynamism) and $v = 28$ m/s (62 mph)*].

At noon in high summer, the sun provides us with about 1,000 W per m^2 on average (meteorologists consider that sunny weather starts from 120 W per m^2). Thereby, a perfect system being able to transform all the solar energy into mechanical energy (far from reality) would require 8 m^2 of solar panels to drive at 62 mph at noon in summer, just considering air friction, which is impossible on a small car.

Actually, the smallest "standard" vehicle can currently produce a power of 50 horsepower, which corresponds to 37,000 W. This power is not only adequate to overcome air friction but also other friction factors (tyre and mechanical friction) but also to provide decent acceleration and climb uphill carrying passengers and luggage (the latest Citroën 2CV or the famous BMC Mini actually produced more than 34 horsepower). Without any storage equipment, in high summer at noon, these two small vehicles would have to be fitted with 37 m^2 of perfect solar panels to produce the same power!

Solar vehicles do exist but they do not correspond to what we commonly call "motor cars". Every year, in Australia, a World Solar Challenge is organized, which is a race between cars running on solar energy. These vehicles are peculiar: small and light, carrying a single passenger and no luggage, with a speed varying according to the amount of sunlight and, of course, running during the day exclusively. This race has existed since 1987 but, if no solar vehicles can be seen on French roads, it is not because petroleum lobbies prevent them from being commercialized, but because the laws of physics will always make it impossible for such vehicles to have the same running specifications as petrol ones. Without any storage device, solar vehicles will never let you drive across France in one day with four people on board and their luggage, even if huge advances allowed for the capture of the whole solar energy reaching the surface of the vehicles.

Likewise, the solar airplane Solar Impulse does not bode well for tomorrow's aviation. A lot of energy will always be necessary to lift a mass, move it and fight against air friction. The surface area of the solar panels required will always be huge compared to the mass of the airplane. It will thus always be difficult, if not impossible, to carry many passengers and their luggage onboard a solar airplane. Research and innovation will not be able to overcome the laws of physics.

Of course, one may imagine vehicles using batteries to store electricity provided only by solar panels, which was actually what Solar Impulse would do. In that case, they would no longer be fully solar vehicles but electric vehicles, the problems of which are well known: low autonomy due to inefficient batteries and electricity production issues (large surface area panels required, unsteady sunlight, environmental impact, opportunity to connect panels to the electric grid in order to mutualize means and favour geographic smoothing etc.).

All these considerations tend to make me think that, so useful and even indispensable as energy efficiency can be, it will not be sufficient. To get a really lower energy consumption, it is necessary to change the use of consuming appliances.

8.3   ENERGY SOBRIETY

Energy sobriety, which consists in giving priority to the most useful uses of energy, "restraining the most extravagant and eliminating harmful ones" [Négawatt, 2011], supposes a definition of the uses that are useful or harmful. Is it "useful" to go and spend a day at the seaside, to go on holiday, to go to the swimming pool, to attend cultural performances or sport events? Is it useful to have a refrigerator, a computer, a dishwasher, a telephone, internet access, a couch, a fitted kitchen? Is it "useful" to provide care to the elderly suffering from serious diseases? Is it "useful" to eat meat or exotic fruit, to drink wine? Is it "useful" to wear nice clothes, to put on make-up, to go to the hairdresser? Is it "useful" to have a shower every day?

It is clear that opinions will vary according to people, particularly those making a living on this "waste", and there are many of them: tourism, culture, sport professionals, domestic appliance, furniture and automobile manufacturers, cattle breeders, winegrowers, webmasters, kitchen fitters, hairdressers, ice-cream or beauty-product vendors etc.

If human beings started harnessing fire, using animal strength, building sailboats, wind or water-mills, it was not just to make money, increase GDP or make shareholders happy, but, above all, because these uses of energy made their life easier. For an even simpler example, when humans started farming and breeding cattle, their aim was to draw more energy (food) compared to what they spent than by having to walk to pick up fruit or chase animals miles away. **A world**

in which energy is scarce is more constraining than a world in which energy is abundant. "Energy can only be spent on healthcare when there is enough net energy left once 'inferior' energy needs (mining, refining, transmitting energy, transporting food, building shelters, providing people with minimum education) have been met" [Court].

Let us imagine some humans shipwrecked on a desert island and have to get by like Robinson Crusoe. It is clear that their lives will be easier if there is an abundant forest on the island than if there are no trees. I am not mentioning wood as a construction material but as an energy source: by burning wood, humans can avoid being cold, cook, get light and make tools, thereby providing for fundamental needs more easily than with less energy.

As we have seen before, beyond a certain energy consumption threshold, the human development index hardly increases and waste appears. Indeed, the consumption of high-tech devices, gadgets, toys, meat, clothes, sodas, alcoholic drinks, ice-creams, jewels, beauty-products, etc., can be reduced without harming our happiness. But I am not sure this waste reduction has a real effect on our energy consumption which is also related to fundamental needs: eating, being accommodated, being safe, moving around, being provided with healthcare etc. All this requires energy. People do not live long where energy consumption is low, as can be observed. Today, development depends on energy.

A report from the United Nations' Environment Programme [Fischer-Kowalski, Swilling] mentions that a scenario allowing just the stabilization of the world's energy consumption and a decrease in greenhouse gas emissions by not more than 40% would induce so many restrictions and would repel so many policy-makers that it can hardly be envisaged as a strategic objective.

8.4   HEAD LICE

A personal anecdote which will surely make some people laugh but which I think is typical of the importance of energy. On a Sunday morning, my wife and I discovered that our children had head lice, which happens in any respectable family. Action stations! I grabbed my phone and gave a call to get the address of the emergency chemist. It was 8 miles away and I drove there to get the stuff that could kill these bugs. We then washed the children's hair and had the washing machine and the tumble dryer work copiously to clean up coats, woolly hats, scarves, bed sheets, cushions, cuddly toys, etc.

Let us now imagine this problem occurring in the marvellous world of Négawatt: I would perhaps not have had a phone, the computerized phone server would not even have existed anyway. It would have taken me at least two hours to ride my bike to and from the pharmacy which may not have been supplied with the products I needed as they are manufactured in energy-hungry factories and transported in energy-greedy lorries. The children's hair may have had to be washed under cold water (the hardest of all!). We would have had to go to the district's collective washing-machine several times or even hand-wash things after heating water, and as the clothes would have had to dry on the line, they would not have been ready for the kids to go to school the next day.

Generations of kids have actually survived nits in a less energy-consuming world, but it was undeniably less convenient. It seems obvious that hygiene is typically easier with hot water and soap. What is less obvious is that hygiene is easier with energy, which is required to pump, heat and depollute water. Energy is required to heat up the oil used to manufacture soap and to build water-delivery infrastructures and sewers, washbasins and bathrooms. Low energy surely means poor hygiene.

9 Money, Too Expensive

There are many discussion topics relating energy to money: carbon taxes, taxes on petroleum products, contribution to electricity public services (CSPE, France), VAT, oil barrel rate, kWh price, regulated fares, nuclear waste dismantling and managing costs, subsidies to renewable energy production, global warming and pollution-related costs, etc.

A few figures: Flamanville's EPR, the very first new-generation nuclear reactor, is expected to cost more than 19 billion euros. The contribution to the electricity public service, which is a tax collected on French electricity bills, allowed for a more than 4.4 billion euro subsidy to renewable energy production systems (mainly wind and solar) for just the year 2016. Adapting renewable energy systems to the French electricity transmission network should cost 33 billion euros. The French state has committed to subsidizing wind and solar energy for a total of 121 billion euros (!) for contracts signed before 2017 at a pace that will go over 7 billion euros for just the year 2025. Germany invested 350 billion euros from 1996 to 2014, i.e. 18 billion per year on average, to support renewable energy. The cost of the solar power station in Noor, Morocco, is estimated at over 8 billion euros. France purchased more than 30 billion euros of crude oil in 2016.

To compare these figures, we should obviously relate them to their use, taking into account installation lifespans, maintenance and storage costs, the necessary adaptations to the grid, dismantling operations, pollution and related diseases, global warming, inflation, immobilized capital, etc. The calculations are so complex that they are always questionable. Nuclear supporters claim that this type of energy is cheaper while opponents say all its related costs are not accounted for.

I have decided not to approach the subject by trying to compare the costs of the various types of energy. Money is so ubiquitous in our society that it is natural to consider it but I leave its related calculations to skilful specialists. **We shall need renewable AND nuclear energy to reduce our consumption in fossil energy.** Opposing them is just not necessarily a good idea.

I think that problems are related to physics before being financial. While it is natural to wonder about the cost of an installation, its technical feasibility should be considered first. If none of the scenarios consider maintaining our energy consumption with just renewable solutions by 2050, it is not just because it would be expensive. The reason is rather that we would not, within a short time, be able to build enough factories to manufacture the necessary materials and machines since we would need a skilled labour force requiring a long time to be trained, because renewable installations have a limited production capacity depending on when the wind blows, because there is no adequate technical solution to the storage problem, because mountains cannot be created to build dams, because trees take a long time to grow, because people do not want wind turbines too close to their homes, because installing wind turbines at sea is really complex. They are physics and human problems and not only financial.

Fossil energy sources and uranium were made available to humans for free by Mother Nature as were wind, sunlight, ocean currents and other renewable sources. Of course miners' wages are to be paid, as they extract coal and uranium, and oil and gas wells managing companies have to be paid, but the people who manufacture, install, supervise, maintain and dismantle renewable energy installations also have to make a living. Of course, an annuity has to be paid to owners of mines and hydrocarbon wells. In both cases, wages and annuities have to be paid [Jancovici Dormez]. Therefore, there is no intrinsic reason for renewable energy to be cheaper, even if some people would like us to believe so by maintaining a confusion between cost and marginal cost (which only accounts for the extra cost due to an extra output).

Fossil energy is not expensive at all compared to the enormous services it renders, i.e. the work it helps us save, thereby the labour we do not have to pay for. Sooner or later, we will have to consume less of it and replacing it will necessarily be very expensive.

Concerning electricity consumption, it is important to keep in mind that wind and photovoltaic sources do not necessarily produce energy when it is needed. Therefore, they should essentially be seen as extra supplies but not as solutions meant to replace other production methods. This would not be the case if the energy produced in excess were stored or reused, which is rarely achieved. More means of production for the same consumption necessarily results in an additional cost!

Germany's situation gives an excellent example: Figure 9.1 shows the evolution of the electrical installed power capacity in Germany from 2002 to 2019. We can

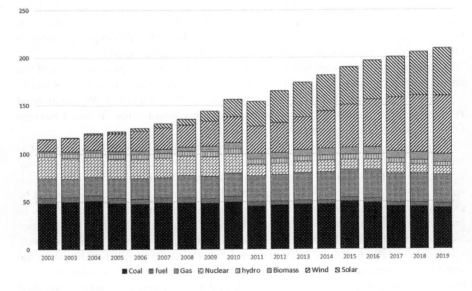

FIGURE 9.1 Evolution of installed power in Germany from 2002 to 2019. (Source: Fraunhofer ISE/AGEE, BMWi, Bundesnetzagentur https://www.energy-charts.de/power_inst.htm.)

observe that while German consumption is steady (it has just increased by 2.5% over the time period), and despite the shutting down of nuclear power stations for 8 GW in 2011, the total installed power capacity has increased considerably, from 115 to 209 GW (+ 82%). The installation of a huge number of wind turbines and solar panels (from 12 to 110 GW) has not reduced the need for other production means: the installed power capacity in controllable power stations (coal, fuel-oil, gas, nuclear, hydraulic, biomass) has gone down from 103 to 99 GW, the installed power capacity in power stations burning fossil energy (coal, fuel-oil, gas) has gone up from 74 to 78 GW. We note that CO_2 emissions did not decrease by more than 15% over the same period while they went down by 18% in France [BP]. I am not saying that wind turbines and solar panels are useless. They help reduce the use of controllable solutions – resulting in lower pollution if fossil energy sources are concerned – but cannot compensate for the partial or complete shutdown of controllable means.

An in-depth study [Burtin-Silva 2015] conducted by Electricité de France's (EDF) R&D department covering 60% of renewable energy production in Europe, including 40% wind and solar installations, concludes that almost the same power should be made available through controllable power stations as that actually supplied by intermittent energy installations. One of the authors, Alain Burtin, declared in 2015:

> On the same day, at the European scale, according to meteorological conditions, we have observed a variability of wind and solar production by around 50% of the European demand. In these conditions, the flexibility of demand and storage capacities cannot replace conventional means of production. Thus, despite the development of 700 GW of variable RES, the required conventional installed capacity does not vary significantly in the scenario compared to the current power.

It would be necessary "to have an additional conventional production capacity of around 500 GW to ensure the security of supply to the European network". Clearly, this study confirms that, even over a large geographical area favourable to smoothing, wind and solar energies come essentially in addition to and not in place of existing production plants. It also shows that, at the European level, such a deployment of renewable energies would make it possible to bring European CO_2 emissions per kWh down to a level close to the current French level.

A doctorate dissertation defended in 2018 and dealing with the "meteorological and climatic potentials and limits of a soothing of renewable energy" [Lassonde] concludes that "minimizing the cost of electricity leads to a small overproduction with important means of storage, while the option of minimizing the total volume of energy stored leads to a strong overproduction involving a price of electricity twice as high". In plain language, it all depends on storage, the huge complexity of which has been considered above.

A report by RTE reads that "relying on wind or solar energy to produce electricity implies a stock of installations with a higher installed power capacity than when relying on controllable power stations" [RTE].

Steven Chu, physics Nobel Prize winner in 1997 and Barack Obama's Secretary of Energy between 2009 and 2013, declared, in 2019: "the electric grid will keep needing controllable installations that can be mobilized on demand" [CHU]. These extra means of production for the same consumption necessarily represent an extra cost for the community, particularly in France where the cost of the amount of uranium saved accounts for a very small proportion of production costs.

These renewable energy installations, whether wind or solar, are financially encouraged. The electricity they inject into the grid has priority even if demand is low when wind and sunlight are present. Buy-back rates are guaranteed by subsidies, creating a niche for investors. Controllable power stations must then lower their power so that production equals consumption. But the problem is that wind and solar installations happen to produce a lot at times when demand is low, which results in falling prices in electricity stock markets. Prices may even be negative sometimes, making some people give money to get rid of their electricity! We might be happy with that and think that it is one step towards free energy but, of course, prices are never negative for the final client. They even increase. Dropping prices on electricity markets make traditional power stations less cost-effective and their owners tend to close them. But, as they are necessary when wind and sunlight are low, "capacity mechanisms" had to be invented in order to subsidize fossil source power stations to prevent them from closing.

> Strange Europe, with an electricity production excess capacity, maintaining massive investment in renewable energy anyway, while wholesale prices fall and retail prices go up to fund the pricing subsidies granted to the more and more numerous renewable energy installations, which results in driving away high electricity consumption firms, thereby increasing overcapacities even more.
>
> **[Bonnaterre]**

What a mess! To support EDF's competitors, a plan called "Regulated Access to Historical Nuclear Energy" (ARENH) even had to be devised, making it mandatory for EDF to sell electricity to alternative suppliers at a fixed rate so that they could sell it back to consumers with an adequate margin. EDF is thus forced to support its competitors!

We might also wonder about this sentence written in ADEME's 2018 report concerning the economic optimization of electric mix [Ademe 2018]: "Too large an extension of historical nuclear energy paired with the development of new renewable energy capacities would keep market prices low and unbalance the cost-effectiveness of all means of production". ADEME hopes for an increase in prices to make renewable energy production cost-effective.

Guaranteed buy-back tariffs for renewable source electricity, Contribution to Electricity Public Services, transmission pricing contribution, capacity mechanisms, Regulated Access to Historical Nuclear Energy, etc.: without fuelling any lengthy debate on liberalization, it seems obvious that patching solutions had to be invented to make way for competition while developing renewable energy production and securing supplies. A free market process does not work in the field of electricity without state mechanisms. The main reason for this is quite simple: as opposed to most other goods and services that we purchase, electricity, which we need permanently, cannot be or can hardly be stored. And, the laws of physics being obstinate, the problem is not likely to be solved soon.

To alleviate these problems, wind and solar electricity should supply new needs as a replacement for fossil energy. For example, we could try to replace oil-fuelled vehicles by electric ones, preferably recharging when these installations supply electricity. We shall perhaps come to that thanks to smart meters allowing consumers to get variable tariffs throughout the day and being able to transmit these tariffs to domestic appliances. But it is anything but simple!

In France, most electricity-producing installations (nuclear reactors) were started up in the 1980s. There has been little investment since and, as expected, these installations are getting old. So, they will have to be either replaced (by what?) or renovated so that they last longer. In any case, it will cost money. It is thus likely that the price of electricity will go up and the price of fossil energy sources is also just as likely to increase, as a result of their increasing scarcity and of rising demand. I hope the price of electricity will rise less quickly than that of fossil energy sources so that the proportion of electricity increases and pollution decreases. But nothing is less certain.

10 Energy Myths and Legends

The development of the internet has probably played a part in the spreading of conspiracy theories and numerous unfounded beliefs. The field of energy is no exception. Articles are regularly published about miraculous technologies producing energy abundantly or helping not to consume any. Energy professionals, petroleum or electricity sellers and all sorts of lobbies are supposed to block the diffusion of such clever inventions. Public research laboratories who can never check the truthfulness of these inventions contradicting the laws of physics would then all be seen as unskilled or in the lobbies' pay. Car manufacturers would have thought hard about the development of electronic injection or hybrid motors to consume less while the water motor would have solved all problems. No small and medium firm would dare market these highly lucrative inventions for fear of lobbies' reprisal. It is ridiculous.

Hydrogen is often presented as a clean energy. Hydrogen vehicles exist and do not release anything other than water: this is true. But there is no, or hardly any, hydrogen in nature. It is currently produced through the transformation of methane, a fossil energy. It can also be produced thanks to electricity, by water electrolysis, thereby providing an energy storage method. Because of inevitable loss, the amount of energy collected is necessarily smaller than that previously used: to collect 1 kWh of electricity, you must have produced 3 and improvement prospects are small. Fuel-cell technology, which transforms hydrogen into electricity, is not new. It was used by NASA to go to the moon. Hydrogen can fuel vehicles, and this technology might be more interesting than the use of batteries, but it doesn't fundamentally change the energy problems. Moreover, as for any energy storage, dangers exist. In that respect, Alain Etienne Beeker, a scientific adviser in charge of energy matters at France Stratégie, wrote in a note in 2004 that "a generalized use of hydrogen under an enormous pressure of 700 bars raises considerable safety problems" [Beeker]. Professor Jacques Foos, who was the director of the nuclear sciences laboratory at *Conservatoire National des Arts et Métiers*, wrote when dealing with hydrogen electric bicycles: "Each bike carries 35 grams of hydrogen. When exploding, these 35 grams of hydrogen release as much energy as almost 1kg of TNT!! Daesh terrorists are amateurs in comparison when they walk around with their explosive belts". "As a citizen who knows a bit about hydrogen-related problems since I was the head of a research lab using this gas, I can't but be outraged by this use" [Foos].

Even better in the same style: the air motor. It works and can move vehicles without pollution, some journalists claim. It is true but the air used has to be compressed, which requires the use of a compressor, which does not work without energy. Again, we are talking about a storage of energy, not about a source, with an important loss.

Some people firmly believe in the water motor. Have a look at the label of a bottle of water: it contains zero calories. If water does not make you put on weight, it is because it contains no calories, in other words, no energy. A water reservoir only represents a certain amount of energy when it is placed high up, the same as for any mass. And we can hardly imagine a huge water tank on top of each vehicle to activate motion as it does for the turbine of a dam (1,200 m³ of water at a height of 3 metres are required to potentially supply the same amount of energy as 1 litre of petrol), unless you manage to get the nuclear energy of water atoms (all atoms have an enormous cohesion energy proportional to their mass). But the reason why nuclear power stations work from uranium and not from water is that we have not been able to so far achieve the nuclear fission of water atoms.

The water motor is often mixed up with the Pantone motor. The idea of this inventor was to use heat from internal combustion engines to create water vapour and inject it into the air inlet in order to reduce the combustion temperature and improve its efficiency. The principle does not seem to be in conflict with the laws of physics since it consists in collecting heat, i.e. energy. Many websites explain how to adapt this system to existing motors. Many DIY enthusiasts claim to have tampered with their cars thereby reducing petrol consumption. Small companies sell kits for some hundred euros claiming to save petrol by injecting water. Some city councils have even installed such systems on their vehicles: Neuilly-Plaisance, Cahors, Vitry-sur-Orne and Calvi gave it a try. But Neuilly Plaisance city council gave it up because "this technique had fouled up engines". It was also abandoned in Cahors, because "the savings were not sufficient to cover the investment" [France Info]. The system is commercialized by none of the car manufacturers. No car manufacturer markets this system. Car manufacturers would therefore miss out on this brilliant invention so as not to attract the wrath of their oil friends or because they are developing electric motors under the pressure of nuclear lobbies. Why would they have other petrol-saving solutions then? Let us keep in mind that the fuel consumption of commercialized vehicles has considerably decreased during recent decades: according to the firm Statista, the average fuel consumption for a French car decreased by 12% between 2004 and 2018. Today's vehicles consume a lot less fuel than the ones of the 1970s although they are a lot heavier. Car manufacturers have significantly improved their engines, so they would obviously use this water-injection system if it was efficient and problem-free. The French Ecology Ministry declared that "to date, no firm proof, regulatory study or trial has been brought to their knowledge demonstrating any saving in terms of fuel-consumption or polluting gas emissions". ADEME, the environment and energy-management agency, confirms that the tests carried out by the French Institute of Science and Technology for Transport, Development and Networks "were not sufficiently conclusive in terms of fuel savings for any further investigation". I contacted Yannick Benard, one of the leaders of the Centre for Technical and Technological Research in Automobile Motors and Acoustics in Bruay-La Buissière (France), on this subject. He explains that "the evolution of motors over the last decades provides, in any case, much higher consumption and pollution gains than that claimed by this system". Therefore, there is no conspiracy that would hide any revolutionary technology from the general public.

The abiotic petroleum theory questions the biological origin of petroleum. Miraculous chemical reactions would allow petroleum pools to self-regenerate as you exploit them. Why should petroleum companies then drill further and deeper to find petroleum under more difficult and costlier extraction conditions?

The Dumas effect: a metal ball plugged into electricity and immersed in water would generate more energy than it consumes. This is actually what is claimed by the French independent inventor, Jean-Christophe Dumas. Such a phenomenon would question the laws of thermodynamics. Being a philanthropist, the inventor published his plans on the internet (https://www.effet-dumas.org). Curiously, I have not heard of any scientific research laboratory publishing anything about this revolution in physics or of any entrepreneur taking on the idea to try and make a fortune. The French magazine "l'Obs" looked into it and questioned thermodynamics specialists. One of them got angry: "It's nothing serious. The protocol is to be laughed at. I will neither waste a single second on this kind of farce nor have my name associated with it". Michel Pons, a thermodynamics expert and director of research, said: "measuring temperatures properly is a difficult thing to do. You have to be a true specialist to avoid any bias and interpreting results is often difficult" [LOBS].

According to some people, vacuum energy had been demonstrated by Nikola Tesla, an engineer. While this scientist actually existed, contributed considerably to the improvement of electric-motor and generator technology and gave his name to a magnetic field unit, he never made energy miraculously appear, as far as I know. He would turn in his grave hearing about all these absurdities reported by people who worship him without understanding what they are talking about.

According to some internet users, Lester Hendershot has developed a motor able to use the Earth's magnetic field. I find it difficult to imagine such a thing, knowing that its amplitude is about 10,000 times lower than that of current electric motors.

Some companies sell "miraculous" systems meant to be able to decrease electricity consumption. Customers are talked into buying them through a supposed patent, but a patent is no guarantee of any efficiency! I personally studied one of them which was promising a reduction on electricity bills. Thanks to capacitors, the system provided actually reduces the electric current flowing in cables by reducing what electricians call reactive power. But this corresponds to energy exchanges, not to consumption. A bill based on active power can only be slightly reduced thanks some slightly lower losses. The technique has been known for a long time and widely used without any miracle system.

If you have time to spare, you may spend hours on the internet trying to understand how these miracle systems work. I wish you luck because everything is done to lose the reader with often incoherent words. I personally gave up. I must be too stupid or have been too well indoctrinated into traditional science. Still, none of the promoters of these miracle energies made a fortune or simply managed to avoid filling up his tank with petrol or paying electricity bills.

11 So, What Should We Do?

Throughout this book, I have tried to explain how complex problems can be and solutions unpleasant or inadequate. I would understand being blamed for criticizing a lot without trying to improve the situation. It is easier to criticize than to act. Nevertheless, I have tried to think about what we can try to do to limit the damage. Here are a few pieces of advice that I would like to give to decision-makers.

11.1 EFFICIENCY AND SOBRIETY

Many actions in favour of energy efficiency have been implemented in recent years in industrial processes, lighting systems, domestic appliances, etc. But the great project that has hardly been initiated is that of housing insulation. Less than 300,000 homes are renovated per year in France, and only 40,000 of which to the low-consumption level. At this pace, it will take at least 100 years, while even not being too demanding about the insulation level, and 750 years for the whole French housing stock to reach "low-consumption" status. Housing is the prime energy consumption entry in France while we are able to build comfortable low-energy consuming homes. It is a huge project, and maximum financial effort should be made.

The problem is more complex regarding transport systems. I doubt large efficiency improvements can be made so that the road vehicles we currently use consume less energy. Sobriety will therefore be required: smaller, lighter, vehicles with less equipment, public transport, bicycles, an economy that would be less dependent on lorries and commuters commuting to work. It is easier said than done when knowing how strongly attached people are to their motor cars and convenient travelling. I admit I do not know how the problem can be tackled politically speaking. Increasing the price of fuels to help behavioural changes is a very delicate decision to make. Drastic and unpopular regulations are likely to be required, such as banning energy-hungry vehicles.

Sobriety will partly be unavoidable if we expect to contribute to the fight against global warming and get ready for a world with less energy. Minds have to be prepared: we will go on holiday less and less in the future, and not so far away, we may not be as warm in winter and hotter in summer, we are likely to have smaller homes, eat less imported food, buy fewer electronic products and have a lower purchasing power.

11.2 TRANSFERRING OIL AND GAS CONSUMPTION TOWARDS ELECTRICITY

Our enemies are oil and gas, as they are often imported, pollute and increase global warming. They are mainly used to travel around and make us warm, which are uses that can be reduced but perhaps not as much as required. It is thus coherent to find solutions to replace oil and gas by electricity. Electric transport systems must thus be developed, whether private or public, whether on rails or roads. The manufacturing of electric cars is definitely energy-greedy but comparative studies on lifecycles show that, if electricity is properly produced, it results in reducing CO_2 emissions by half.

To heat buildings and water, electricity results in lower pollution than gas in countries where fossil fuels are little used. Moreover, heat-pump technology is up and running. They are systems running on the same principle as refrigerators, able to collect calories from outside, from the ground or unconfined groundwater, and allowing people to be warm while consuming two or three times less electricity than with conventional heating systems.

11.3 PRODUCING ELECTRICITY THANKS TO CONTROLLABLE AND LOW-POLLUTION METHODS

Transferring oil and gas consumption to electricity is only relevant if electricity is produced without any fossil energy. Nuclear and hydraulic installations currently supply 80% of French electricity in an extremely efficient way: little pollution of any kind, low greenhouse gas emissions, little impact on health, few power cuts and a kWh price amongst the cheapest in Europe! But why would we want to change everything while this centralized system works very well? French nuclear reactors were mostly started up in the 1980s. They will be 50 years old in 2030 so their replacement is to be planned. Building new reactors will certainly not be an easy thing but it is necessary if we do not want to rely on gas. Part of our future electricity consumption, particularly that from electric vehicles, can be supplied by wind energy providing that consumption can be controlled. As a matter of fact, battery recharges and some uses of electricity can sometimes be postponed. The major drawback with wind energy, which is its lack of control, can then be toned down and the use of controllable power stations reduced. This will require more fluctuating tariffs varying according to electricity demand and supply, encouraging consumers to adapt via smart meters. The same reasoning could be applied to solar electricity, but I am a lot more doubtful about it because of its environmental impact and its poor energy return rate. In some countries, hydroelectricity will play a more important part.

11.4 DEVELOPING THERMAL RENEWABLE ENERGY SYSTEMS

When we talk about renewable energies, we immediately think of wind and photovoltaic, the major drawback of which being that the amount of electricity they supply depends on weather conditions and is difficult to store. Other renewable energies do not have this drawback and seem more relevant to me. Thermal solar energy, with simple pipes through which a heat-transfer fluid circulates, supplies heat that can be easily stored for a few hours, for example in a hot-water tank. Wood and biogas can obviously be stored directly and usefully replace fossil fuel and gas boilers. Deep-drilling geothermal energy has undoubtedly still a large potential to supply heat networks or to be associated with heat-pumps. I may have left out technologies that might be relevant.

12 Conclusion, Prospects

At the risk of repeating myself, I maintain that no French energy transition scenario claims that fossil and nuclear energy can be replaced by renewable energy, unless consumption is considerably reduced.

The energy-efficiency lever wins unanimous support since it means consuming less for the provision of an equal service. The laws of physics and the recent history of technological advances show that this necessary lever will not be sufficient.

Energy sobriety is far more complex to develop as it implies considerable lifestyle and changes in the way society is organized. Energy consumption has allowed for the replacement of humans by machines and a tertiarization of economy. Less energy means less transport, fewer machines, less medical care, less heat, less comfort, less food, fewer homes or even less education or culture. Less energy means more thankless tasks, thereby more work and perhaps even more jobs, but paradoxically fewer human activities, fewer goods and service exchanges, thus less wealth. Sobriety and poverty are close concepts.

Unexpected technological innovations could perhaps come to light and be a game-changer, but I do not see currently which miracle technology would be ready soon enough as we shall be short of oil and gas before the next century and the various sources of pollution and global warming are urgent issues. The laws of physics are unavoidable, and their limits will not be pushed back by future technological advances. Indeed, some of the laws of physics accepted by the scientific community at the beginning of the 20th century were questioned by Einstein, but relying on a revolution of these laws to solve these huge issues seems rather hazardous.

I think that some people's optimism, based on the belief that human intelligence and technology will manage to find a solution to all these issues, is due to a basic ignorance of physics. Sometimes, the same people even criticize science and technology while they are blindly confident in them to find miracle solutions.

Humans have been able to do extraordinary things, to modify their environment while no other animal species has managed to do so, and to resolve huge problems. True, but with the use of ever more energy!

Creating tools, building comfortable homes and schools, developing the telegraph and then the telephone, producing food for billions of human beings and ensuring its preservation, manufacturing domestic appliances, hygiene products, bicycles, motorcars, trains, amazing airplanes allowing people to fly across the planet, going to the moon, fighting epidemics, creating radio and TV sets, cinema, stadiums and theatre halls, computers, GPS devices, self-driving cars, weather forecast systems, developing the internet, sending images thousands of miles away in a fraction of a second, carrying out heart transplants, making spectacles, hip prostheses, scanners, elevators, etc. All this is definitely fabulous! But it all requires more and more energy! None of it is thus sustainable, and I think this fact of life is just unavoidable today.

It is a fact that I personally find rather difficult to admit as I have always admired science, technology, human intelligence and the huge advances they have achieved.

Before long, a shortage in fossil energy sources will necessarily occur, and renewable or nuclear energy will not make up for their replacement. If only our consumption were constant. The annual increase of the world population and energy consumption is roughly equal to one more France every year! For each of the ten billion human beings by 2050 to have access to only half of a French person's current energy consumption, world energy consumption would have to be increased by 40%. Limiting reproduction is not a natural measure for living beings who always want to "be fruitful and multiply". But it is clear that an increase in population will amplify problems and require sharing limited resources between a larger number of humans, which implies getting less each.

Policy makers have three possibilities for the decades to come:

- Consuming much less energy. This means reorganising societies completely, which people will find difficult to agree on. Some suggest a more sober society, but I would say a poorer society. It is impossible to live the way we live in rich countries while consuming little energy. And people living in countries consuming little energy often wish they could consume more. Policy makers hardly seem likely to be elected democratically while promoting energy sobriety. It does not just mean doing without the latest generation smartphone, tablet, TV set, spa, luxury car, a week-end at the seaside or a holiday on remote islands.

    The consequence of a shortage in energy will affect housing, health, education, nutrition, culture, etc. Economic and social consequences can be so huge that the risk of rebellion and wars cannot be denied. Energy and growth have always been related. I doubt that reducing energy consumption would not result in economic degrowth, which means becoming poorer. Getting an adequate piece of the pie is more difficult when its size decreases, and even more so if there are more of us.

- Developing nuclear energy. Nuclear energy can obviously be dangerous, but it is less so than fossil sources or a lack of energy. I think that the benefit to risk ratio is largely in its favour and that we will not face as many problems using it than not. Nuclear energy is not a miracle solution facing the huge issues we have evoked. As with renewable energy sources, it will be some compensation for the energy shortage and a way to be less dependent on fossil sources. Yet, it will not be possible to develop nuclear everywhere and at a sufficient pace to make up for the missing energy. Problems will be huge with or without nuclear energy. In a far future, it may supply an important part of human beings' energy, but not in the coming decades. But, as the views antinuclear activists express are easier to understand and more largely covered by media than what professionals may explain, I doubt nuclear energy will significantly develop.

- Carrying on exploiting fossil energy sources – particularly coal, non-conventional oils and shale gas – since resources exist, thereby increasing pollution and global warming with such consequences as respiratory diseases, floods, storms, etc. I would not be surprised if humans endeavour to collect all the coal, gas and oil they can extract through energy cost-effective means. These energies are too incredibly convenient and easy to use to decide to do without. Renewable energy sources were exploited long before fossil ones. As the latter allowed humans to progress as never before, they will not give them up before they are forced to do so by the laws of physics. Global warming and pollution have still got good days ahead.

As fossil resources are inevitably due to dwindle, renewable and nuclear energy sources will not soon be ready to replace them adequately, and as energy efficiency has limits, our problems are obviously going to get worse. Here is a pessimistic view which is important to be aware of if we hope to carry on living in peace and democracy. It is useless to blame the ruling policy makers if they do not improve their citizens' purchasing power and living standard. The cause does not necessarily lie in their incompetence, corruption or lack of will, it is also related to the laws of physics against which they are powerless. Enjoying high purchasing power means spending more energy. Increasing or decreasing interest rates, creating money or fighting against inflation does not change physics. After the 2008 crisis, billions were found to save banks because it just meant changing figures in some computer programs, but energy cannot be managed that way.

I happened to hear that renewable energy, LED lightbulbs, vegetarianism, organic farming, vegetable gardens, local currencies, composting, recycling, car-sharing, everyday little actions, anti-waste behaviours, etc., will help us live in happiness. I have nothing against these ideas which will certainly smooth the rough edges. I only use low-energy lightbulbs, I do not eat much meat and I conscientiously sort my waste, but I doubt these ideas will change the orders of magnitude. I observe that they often stem from rich countries' inhabitants who, even when being careful, depend a lot on energy. The people who already live in real sobriety are generally looking forward to the end of it. Many people who imagine themselves happy in a sober world do not realise what this world will be like. Of course, it all depends on what we call happiness, such a broad debate. I hold the conviction that energy does not make happiness but that it is a great help.

Bibliography

[Académie] Académie des Technologies, *Trajectoires d'évolution du mix électrique 2020-2060, commentaires d'une étude Ademe publiée le 10 décembre 2018*, janvier 2019.

[Ademe 2013] ADEME, *Contribution de l'ADEME à l'élaboration de visions énergétiques 2030-2050. Synthèse avec évaluation macro-économique*, 2013.

[Ademe 2015] ADEME, *Un mix électrique 100 % renouvelable ? Analyses et optimisations*, 2015.

[Ademe 2017] ADEME, *Actualisation du scénario énergie-climat, ADEME 2030-2050*, 2017.

[Ademe 2018] ADEME, *Trajectoires d'évolution du mix électrique 2020-2060*, 2018.

[Ancre] Agence Nationale de Coordination de la Recherche pour l'Energie, *Scénarios de l'ANCRE pour la transition énergétique*, 2013.

[Auzanneau] Mathieu Auzanneau, *Or noir. La grande histoire du pétrole*, La Découverte, 2015. *Oil, Power and War: A Dark History*, Chelsea Green Publishing, 2018

[Barré] Bertrand Barré, *Le Nucléaire, débats et réalités*, Ellipses, 2011.

[Basdevant] Jean-Louis Basdevant, *Maîtriser le nucléaire*, Eyrolles, 2012.

[Beeker] Etienne Beeker, *Y a-t-il une place pour l'hydrogène dans la transition énergétique ?*, note d'analyse de France Stratégie n°15, Aout 2014.

[Bellal] Amar Bellal, Jeremy Rifkin, le nouveau prophète de l'énergie de l'industrie du Nord-Pas-de-Calais, https://environnement-energie.org/

[Ben Ahmed] Hamid Ben Hamed, Bernard Multon, Yaël Thiaux, Consommation d'énergie, ressources énergétiques et place de l'électricité, *Techniques de l'ingénieur*, d3900, 2011.

[Bihouix low tech] Philippe Bihouix, *L'Âge des low-tech. Vers une civilisation techniquement soutenable*, Éditions du Seuil, 2014.

[Bihouix myth] Philippe Bihouix, Du mythe de la croissance "verte" à un monde post-croissance, extrait de *Crime climatique, stop !*, Éditions du Seuil 2015. http://rue89bordeaux.com/2015/09/du-mythe-de-la-croissance-verte-a-un-monde-post-croissance/

[Bonnaterre] Raymond Bonnaterre, Puissance électrique intermittente éolienne et photovoltaïque en Allemagne : simulation simplifiée d'écrêtage des pointes, *Techniques de l'ingénieur*, mai 2014.

[BL] BL évolution, Comment s'aligner sur une trajectoire compatible avec les 1,5°, Février 2019.

[BP] *BP statistical review of world energy 2016*, BP, 2017, http://www.bp.com/en/global/corporate/energy-economics/statistical-review-of-world-energy.html

[Bréon SPS] François Marie-Bréon, La problématique de l'énergie dans les rapports du GIEC, *revue Sciences et pseudo-sciences n° 329*, juillet-septembre 2019, pp 23-26.

[Burtin-Silva 2015] Alain Burtin, Vera Silva, EDF, Technical and economic analysis of the European system with 60 % RES, 2015.

[Carminel] Thierry Carminel, L'impossible découplage entre énergie et croissance, http://decroissance.blog.lemonde.fr/2013/06/16/impossible-decouplage/

[CEW] Clean Energy Wire, *Germany's three lignite mining regions*, https://www.cleanenergywire.org/factsheets/germanys-three-lignite-mining-regions

[CGDD 135] Commissariat Général au Développement Durable, publication n° 135, *Un habitat plus compact et moins énergivore : pour quels coûts de construction ?* , décembre 2015.

[Charlez] Philippe Charlez, *Croissance, énergie, climat, dépasser la quadrature du cercle*, Deoeck supérieur, 2017

[CHU] Steven Chu, *La transition énergétique ne va pas assez vite*, journal Le Monde du 5 octobre 2019.

[Clack] Christopher T.M. Clack, Staffan A. Qvist, Jay Apt, Morgan Bazilian, Adam R. Brandt, Ken Caldeira, Steven J. Davis, Victor Diakov, Mark A. Handschy, Paul D.H. Hines, Paulina Jaramillo, Daniel M. Kammen, Jane C.S. Long, M. Granger Morgan, Adam Reed, Varun Sivaram, James Sweeney, George R. Tynan, David G. Victor, John P. Weyant, Jay F. Whitacre, Evaluation of a proposal for reliable low-cost grid power with 100 % wind, water, and solar, *Proceedings of the National Academy of Sciences of the United States of America*, doi: 10.1073/pnas.1610381114, 2016.

[Cochet] Yves Cochet, *Pétrole apocalypse*, Fayard, 2005.

[Convention ampoules] Ministère de l'Écologie, de l'Énergie, du Développement durable et de l'Aménagement du territoire, Convention sur le retrait de la vente des ampoules à incandescence et la promotion des lampes basse consommation, 2008.

[Court] Victor Court, Énergie nette et EROI (*Energy Return On Investment*). Une autre approche de la transition énergétique, *Informations et Débats*, n° 40, octobre 2015, chaire Économie du climat de l'université de Paris-Dauphine.

[Datalab climat] Commissariat général au développement durable, *Chiffres clés du climat*, Ministère de la transition écologique et solidaire, Datalab édition 2019.

[Datalab énergie] Commissariat général au développement durable, *Chiffres clés de l'énergie*, Ministère de la transition écologique et solidaire, Datalab Septembre 2019.

[Diamond] Jared Diamond, *Collapse: How Societies Choose to Fail or Succeed*, 2005.

[Durand] Bernard Durand, Dangers et risques, une comparaison de la radioactivité et de la pollution atmosphérique, *European Scientist*, 2018.

[EDK] Europe's Dark Cloud. How coal-burning countries are making their neighbours sick, WWF, HEAL, CAN Europe, Sandbag, 2016.

[Efficiency-N] André Berger; Tom Blees; Francois-Marie Breon; Barry W. Brook; Marc Deffrennes; Bernard Durand; Philippe Hansen; Elisabeth Huffer; Ravi B. Grover; Claude Guet; Weiping Liu; Frederic Livet; Herve Nifenecker; Michel Petit; Gérard Pierre; Henri Prévot; Sébastien Richet; Henri Safa; Massimo Salvatores; Michael Schneeberger; Bob Wornan; Suyan Zhou, Nuclear energy and bio energy carbon capture and storage, keys for obtaining 1.5°C mean surface temperature limit, *International Journal of Global Energy Issues* Vol.40 No.3/4, 2017, DOI: 10.1504/IJGEI.2017.10007761

[EHJ] Jos Lelieveld, Klaus Klingmüller, Andrea Pozzer, Ulrich Pöschl, Mohammed Fnais, Andreas Daiber, Thomas Münzel, Cardiovascular disease burden from ambient air pollution in Europe reassessed using novel hazard ratio functions, *European Heart Journal*, Volume 40, Issue 20, 21 May 2019, Pages 1590–1596, https://doi.org/10.1093/eurheartj/ehz135

[Empreinte] Commissariat général au développement durable, *L'empreinte carbone, les émissions cachées de notre consommation*, novembre 2015.

[EU Energy] European Commission, *EU energy in figures*, statistical pocketbook 2019.

[Finon SPS] Dominique Finon, Les conséquences d'un tout renouvelable pour la production d'électricité, *revue Sciences et pseudo-sciences n° 329*, juillet-septembre 2019, pp 52-57.

[Fischer-Kowalski, Swilling] Fischer-Kowalski M., Swilling M., Decoupling natural resource use and environmental impacts from economic growth, United Nations Environment Program, 2011.

[Fizaine] Florian Fizaine, Victor Court, Energy expenditure, economic growth, and the minimum EROI of society, *Energy Policy. The International Journal of Political, Economic, Planning, Environmental and Social Aspects of Energy*, n° 95, p. 172-186, 2016.
http://dx.doi.org/10.1016/j.enpol.2016.04.039.

[Foos] Jacques Foos, Chroniques du 20Ie siècle - *Regard sur la société d'aujourd'hui pour préparer efficacement celle de demain !*, Editions HD, 2019.

[France info] à propos du moteur Pantone, https://www.francetvinfo.fr/economie/transports/prix-des-carburants/non-on-ne-vous-cache-pas-la-verite-sur-le-moteur-a-eau-qui-rendrait-les-voitures-plus-propres_3035893.html

[Gadrey] Jean Gadrey, *Adieu à la croissance. Bien vivre dans un monde solidaire*, Éditions Les petits matins, 2010.

[Gadrey blog] Jean Gadrey, Jeremy Rifkin, le gourou du gotha européen, blog d'*Alternatives économiques*.
http://alternatives-economiques.fr/blogs/gadrey/2013/05/09/jeremy-rifkin-le-gourou-du-gotha-europeen-1/

[GEO] Global Electrification, Fukushima : peu ou pas d'impact des radiations sur la santé humaine, *Lettre géopolitique de l'électricité*, n° 61, 20 mars 2016.

[Giraud interview] Gaël Giraud, interview sur le blog Oil Man de Mathieu Auzanneau, http://petrole.blog.lemonde.fr/2014/04/19/gael-giraud-du-cnrs-le-vrai-role-de-lenergie-va-obliger-les-economistes-a-changer-de-dogme/

[Giraud Kahraman] Gaël Giraud, Zeynep Kahraman, How dependent is output growth on primary energy ?, Séminaire de l'École d'économie de Paris organisé avec le concours du Commissariat général au développement durable, 2014.

[Grand] Dominique Grand, Christian Le Brun, Roland Vidil, Un mix électrique à 100 % renouvelable : avec quelles conséquences ?, *La Revue de l'énergie*, n° 631, mai-juin 2016.

[Greenpeace 2013] Greenpeace, *Scénario de transition énergétique*, 2013.

[HCC] Haut Conseil pour le Climat, premier rapport annuel, juin 2019.

[Heinberg] Richard Heinberg, *The Party's Over: Oil, War, and the Fate of Industrial Societies*, Clairview Books, 2005.

[IEA] International Energy Agency, Key World Energy Statistics, 2017.

[IEA nuclear power] International Energy Agency, Nuclear Power in a Clean Energy System", mai 2019.

[IPCC-III] Technology-specific Cost and Performance Parameters, Annexe III du 5ème rapport du GIEC-IPCC, 2014.

[IPCC 2014 GT III] Contribution du groupe de travail iii au cinquième rapport d'évaluation du groupe d'experts intergouvernemental sur l'évolution du climat, Changements climatiques, L'atténuation du changement climatique, Résumé à l'intention des décideurs, 2014.

[IPCC 2018] Intergovernmental Panel on Climate Change, Global warming of 1,5°C, Summary for Policymakers, 2018.

[Jackson] Tim Jackson, *Prosperity Without Growth: Economics for a Finite Planet*, 2009.

[Jancovici Dormez] Jean-Marc Jancovici, *Dormez tranquille jusqu'en 2100, et autres malentendus sur le climat et l'énergie*, Odile Jacob, 2005.

[Jancovici Le plein] Jean-Marc Jancovici, Alain Grandjean, *Le plein, s'il vous plaît !*, Éditions du Seuil, 2006.

[Jancovici Web] Jean-Marc Jancovici, www.manicore.com. Sur le lien entre énergie et PIB : http://www.manicore.com/documentation/energie.html.

[Jouanno] Chantal Jouanno, L'efficacité énergétique dans l'Union européenne. Panorama des politiques et des bonnes pratiques, Service Observation, économie et évaluation de l'ADEME, p. 1-52, 2008.

[Kharecha Hansen] Pushker A. Kharecha et James E. Hansen, Prevented mortality and greenhouse gas emissions from historical and projected nuclear power, *Environmental Science and Technology*, dx.doi.org/10.1021/es3051197l Environ. Sci. Technol., 47, 4889-4895, 2013.

[Koch] Franz H. Koch, *Hydropower-Internalized Costs and Externalized Benefits*, International Energy Agency (IEA) - Implementing Agreement for Hydropower Technologies and Programs, Ottawa, Canada, 2000.

[Kuo] Way Kuo, *Fiabilité de l'énergie renouvelable et nucléaire*, Éditions ISTE, 2015.

[Lassonde] Sylvain Lassonde, *Potentiels et limites météorologiques et climatiques d'un foisonnement des énergies renouvelables*, thèse de Doctorat de l'Université Paris-Saclay soutenue le 21 juin 2018.

[Livet] Frédéric Livet, *L'Effet de l'accident de Fukushima sur la production et la consommation d'électricité du Japon*, Association Sauvons le climat, 2013.

[LOBS], à propos de l'effet Dumas, https://www.nouvelobs.com/rue89/rue89-planete/2014 1205.RUE6891/l-effet-dumas-l-energie-miracle-qui-ne-marche-que-sur-facebook .html

[Markandya Wilkinson] Anil Markandya et Paul Wilkinson, Electricity generation and health, *The Lancet*, vol. 370, p. 979-990, 2007.

[Master TRI] Conseil régional Nord-Pas-de-Calais, Master plan de troisième révolution industrielle de la région Nord-Pas-de-Calais, 2013.

[McDonald] Robert I. McDonald, Joseph Fargione, Joe Kiesecker, William M. Miller, Jimmie Powell, Energy Sprawl or Energy Efficiency: Climate Policy Impacts on Natural Habitat for the United States of America, Plosone, August 2009, volume 4, Issue 8.

[Meadows] Donella Meadows, Denis Meadows, Jorgen Randers, *The Limits to Growth, the 30 year update*, Éditions Rue de l'Échiquier, 2004.

[Mix] Commissariat général au développement durable, Chiffres et statistiques, L'évolution du mix électrique dans le monde entre 1980 et 2010, avril 2013.

[Mouhot] Jean-François Mouhot, *Des esclaves énergétiques*, Éditions Champ Vallon, 2011.

[Mourik] Maarten Van Mourik and Oskar Slingerland, *The misunderstood crisis*, l'Artilleur, 2014.

[Musolino] Michel Musolino, *L'Économie pour les nuls*, 3e édition, Éditions First.

[Negatep] Claude Acket, Hubert Flocard, Claude Jeandron, Hervé Nifenecker, Henry Prévot, Jean-Marie Seiler, *Diviser par quatre les rejets de CO_2 dus à l'énergie : le scénario Négatep*, Association Sauvons le climat, 2017.

[Négawatt 2011] Association Négawatt, Scénario Négawatt 2011, 2011.

[Négawatt 2017] Association Négawatt, Scenario Négawatt 2017-2050, 2017.

[NégaWatt Hypothèses] Association NégaWatt, Scénario négaWatt 2017-2050, Hypothèses et résultats, 2018.

[Oil man] Mathieu Auzanneau, blog consacré au pétrole, http://petrole.blog.lemonde.fr/

[WHO Chernobyl] *Effets sanitaires de l'accident de Tchernobyl*, 2006, http://www.who.int/ mediacentre/factsheets/fs303/fr/

[Pitron] Guillaume Pitron, *la guerre des métaux rares*, éditions Les liens qui libèrent, 2018 / *The war of rare metals: The hidden side of the green energy and digital transition*, Scribe Publications 2021.

[Rabl Spadaro] A. Rabl & J.V. Spadaro, Les coûts externes de l'électricité, *Revue de l'énergie*, n° 525, p. 151-163, mars-avril 2001.

[Raugei] Marco Raugei, Enrica Leccisi, A comprehensive assessment of the energy perfor-
  mance of the full range of electricity generation technologies deployed in the United
  Kingdom, *Energy Policy*, vol. 90, March 2016, p. 46-59. doi: 10.1016/j.enpol.2015.12.011
[Rifkin] Jeremy Rifkin, *The Third industrial revolution*, 2011.
[RTE] Réseau de transport de l'électricité, *Les Enjeux du développement du réseau. Schéma
  décennal de développement du réseau de transport de l'électricité*, édition 2015.
[RTE BP 2017] Réseau de transport de l'électricité, *Bilan prévisionnel de l'équilibre offre-
  demande d'électricité en France*, édition 2017.
[Sapy] Georges Sapy, Les énergies intermittentes mettent-elles en cause la stabilité des
  réseaux ?, *revue Sciences et pseudo-sciences n° 329*, juillet-septembre 2019, pp 47-51.
[Systèmes] *Les systèmes électriques de demain*, éditions Lavoisier, 2018.
[Sorin] Francis Sorin, *Déchets nucléaires : où est le problème ?*, EDP Sciences, 2015.
[Sourrouille] Michel Sourrouille, *Moins nombreux, plus heureux. L'urgence écologique*,
  Éditions Sang de la terre, 2014.
[SPS 329] Energie et climat... rien n'est simple, *revue Sciences et pseudo-sciences n° 329*,
  juillet-septembre 2019.
[Treiner SPS] Jacques Treiner, Combien d'énergie pour produire de l'énergie, revue Sciences
  et pseudo-sciences n° 329, juillet-septembre 2019, pp 23-26.
[Thévard] Benoît Thévard, La diminution de l'énergie nette, frontière ultime de
  l'Anthropocène, Institut Momentum, séminaire du 13 décembre 2013.
[UNSCEAR] Report of the United Nations Scientific Committee on the Effects of Atomic
  Radiation to the General Assembly, Sources, effects and risks of ionizing radiation,
  2013.
[VIDAL] Olivier VIDAL , *Mineral Resources and Energy, Future Stakes in Energy
  Transition,* Elsevier, 2018.
[Weissbach] D. Weißbach, G. Ruprecht, A. Huke, K. Czerski, S. Gottlieb, A. Hussein, Energy
  intensities, EROIs (energy returned on invested), and energy payback times of electric-
  ity generating power plants, *Energy*, vol. 52, p. 210-221, April 2013.
http://dx.doi.org/10.1016/j.energy.2013.01.029
[WEO] World Energy Outlook 2014, International Energy Agency, 2014.
[wiki Fukushima] Wikipédia, Conséquences sanitaires et sociales de l'accident nucléaire de
  Fukushima.
https://fr.wikipedia.org/wiki/Cons %C3 %A9quences_sanitaires_et_sociales_de_l'accide
  nt_nucl %C3 %A9aire_de_Fukushima#Mesures_de_protection_pour_la_population
[Wingert] Jean-Luc Wingert, *La Vie après le pétrole*, Autrement, coll. Frontières, 2005.
[World Bank] World Bank Group, The growing role of minerals and metals for a low carbon
  future, 2017.
[Wynes] Seth Wines, Kimberly A. Nicholas, The climate mitigation gap : education and gov-
  ernment recommendations miss the most effective individual actions, *Environmental
  Research Letters*, vol. 12, n° 7, 2017. https://doi.org/10.1088/1748-9326/aa7541
[WWS] Mark Z. Jacobson, Mark A. Delucchi, Mary A. Cameron, Bethany A. Frew, Low-
cost solution to the grid reliability problem with 100 % penetration of intermittent wind,
water, and solar for all purposes, *Proceedings of the National Academy of Sciences of the
United States of America*, vol. 112, n° 49, December 8, 2015.

Index

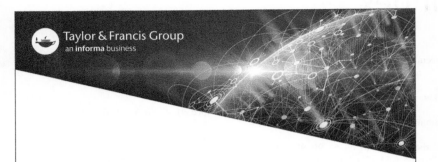

For Product Safety Concerns and Information please contact our EU
representative GPSR@taylorandfrancis.com Taylor & Francis Verlag GmbH,
Kaufingerstraße 24, 80331 München, Germany

Printed and bound by CPI Group (UK) Ltd, Croydon, CR0 4YY
08/06/2025
01897007-0012